NORTHUMBERLAND
Travel Guide 2025-2026

Discover Timeless Castles, Rugged Coastlines, Hidden Villages, and Epic Roman Trails in England's Wild Northeast

Jennifer Segura

Copyright © 2025 by Jennifer Segura

All rights reserved. No part of this publication may be reproduced, distributed, or transmitted in any form or by any means, electronic, mechanical, photocopying, recording, or otherwise, without the prior written permission of the author, except in the case of brief quotations used in reviews, articles, or critical analyses.

Disclaimer

This book is meant to help you plan your trip and make the most of your travel experience. The places, prices, times, and other details shared in this guide were correct when written, but things can change. Please check the latest information before you go.

This book is based on the author's personal experiences and research. It is not meant to replace advice from local experts, travel professionals, or official sources.

The author and publisher are not responsible for any changes, delays, losses, or problems that may happen during your trip. Travel comes with risks, and it's always best to plan carefully and stay informed.

Northumberland Travel Guide 2025-2025

Northumberland Travel Guide 2025-2025

TABLE OF CONTENTS

Introduction.. 8
    *Welcome to Northumberland......................................*8
    *Why Northumberland?..*9
    What Makes It a Hidden Gem................................ 10
    *How to Use This Guide...*10
    Fun Facts You Didn't Know About Northumberland. 11

Chapter 1: Planning Your Northumberland Adventure.. 13
    *When to Visit (Seasons & Weather).........................*14
    Getting There: Trains, Buses, Airports & Car Hire 15
    *Getting Around: Public Transport, Driving, and Walking..*17
    Local Customs & Travel Etiquette......................... 18
    *Safety Tips and Emergency Contacts.....................*19
    *Currency, Costs & Budgeting Tips...........................*19
    *What to Pack: Year-Round Essentials....................*20

Chapter 2: Top 10 Must-See Attractions........... 21
    Bamburgh Castle: Fortress by the Sea.................... 23
    Alnwick Castle & Gardens: Harry Potter and More.. 28
    *Hadrian's Wall & Sycamore Gap: Walking With Romans...*34
    *Holy Island of Lindisfarne: Tides and Tranquility*39
    Dunstanburgh Castle Coastal Walk: Ruins and Rolling Waves.. 45
    *Farne Islands: Puffins, Seals & Boat Trips..............*50
    Craster Village & Kippers: A Taste of the Sea........ 55
    Northumberland National Park: The Wild Heart. 59

Kielder Water & Observatory: Dark Sky Magic.... 64
Warkworth Village & Castle: A Medieval Jewel on the Coquet.............. 68

Chapter 3: Northumberland's Enchanted Castles.. 73
Chillingham Castle: The Most Haunted in Britain. 74
Prudhoe Castle: Off-the-Beaten Path...................... 75
Etal & Norham Castles: Border Strongholds......... 77
Belsay Hall and Castle: Grand Estates & Gardens 78

Chapter 4: Roman Britain & Ancient Trails.... 81
Walking Hadrian's Wall Path: Day-by-Day Guide... 82
Vindolanda Fort & Live Archaeology..................... 84
Roman Museums & History Hotspots.................... 86

Chapter 5: Coastal Escapes & Seaside Towns. 88
Seahouses: Boat Tours, Shops & Chips................... 89
Beadnell Bay: Water Sports & Windswept Beauty 90
Alnmouth: Colorful Cottages and Artists' Haven... 91
Berwick-upon-Tweed: Border Town with Scottish Soul.. 92
Druridge Bay Country Park...................................... 93

Chapter 6: Hidden Villages & Market Towns.. 94
Rothbury: Gateway to the Cheviots........................ 95
Wooler: A Hiker's Haven... 96
Amble: Seafood & the Harbour Village.................. 97
Hexham: Abbey, Arts, and Riverside Charm......... 98
Haltwhistle: The Centre of Britain........................ 99

Chapter 7: Nature, Parks & Stargazing...........101
Northumberland National Park: Wildlife & Walks... 102

The Cheviot Hills: Best Trails & Panoramas........ 103
Kielder Forest: Bike Trails & Adventure............... 104
Hauxley Wildlife Discovery Centre....................... 104
Dark Sky Discovery Sites: Where and When........ 105

Chapter 8: Outdoor Adventures for All........... 107
Best Walks for Families, Seniors, and Serious Hikers.. 108
Coastal Walks with Wheelchair Access................. 109
Cycling Routes for All Levels................................ 109
Kayaking, Surfing, and Paddleboarding............... 110
Horse Riding Experiences...................................... 111

Chapter 9: Food, Pubs & Local Delights.......... 113
Best Places for Seafood: Craster, Seahouses & Amble... 113
Top Traditional Northumbrian Dishes to Try...... 114
Historic Pubs with Real Ale and Ghost Stories..... 115
Afternoon Tea Spots & Farm Shops...................... 116
Local Markets and Food Festivals......................... 116

Chapter 10: Accommodation for Every Budget... 118
Historic Inns and Boutique Hotels........................ 118
Budget B&Bs and Hostels...................................... 120
Romantic Stays and Coastal Cottages................... 121
Family-Friendly Resorts and Holiday Parks........ 123
Glamping, Camping, and Eco-Lodges................... 124

Chapter 11: Itineraries to Suit Every Traveler.... 127
3 Days in Northumberland: A Quick Escape........ 127
7-Day Classic Northumberland............................ 128

Romantic Getaway for Couples............................ 130
Family Fun Itinerary with Kids............................131
Senior-Friendly Relaxed Journey........................ 132
Backpacker's Budget Itinerary............................133
Photographer's Trail: Castles, Wildlife, and Landscapes.. 134

Chapter 12: Northumberland for Every Season.. 136

Spring: Blossoms, Birds & Coastal Breezes.......... 136
Summer: Festivals, Hikes & Sea Adventures........ 137
Autumn: Foliage, Peace & Stargazing................... 138
Winter: Snowy Castles, Quiet Trails & Firelit Pubs... 139

Chapter 13: Events, Festivals & Local Traditions 140

Alnwick Garden Illuminations............................ 140
Lindisfarne Gospels Festival................................ 141
Farne Islands Puffin Watch (May–July).............. 143
Northumberland County Show............................ 144
Berwick Film & Media Arts Festival......................145
Local Christmas Markets..145

Chapter 14: Day Trips Beyond Northumberland 147

Durham & Cathedral Day Trip..............................147
Edinburgh from Berwick-upon-Tweed................. 148
Hadrian's Wall & The Lake District Border..........149
Tynemouth & Newcastle Coastal Break................149

Exclusive Bonus.. 151
Conclusion.. 155
Maps.. 157

Northumberland Travel Guide 2025-2025

KINDLY REFER TO THE MAP SECTION GO ACCESS THE INTERACTIVE MAPS

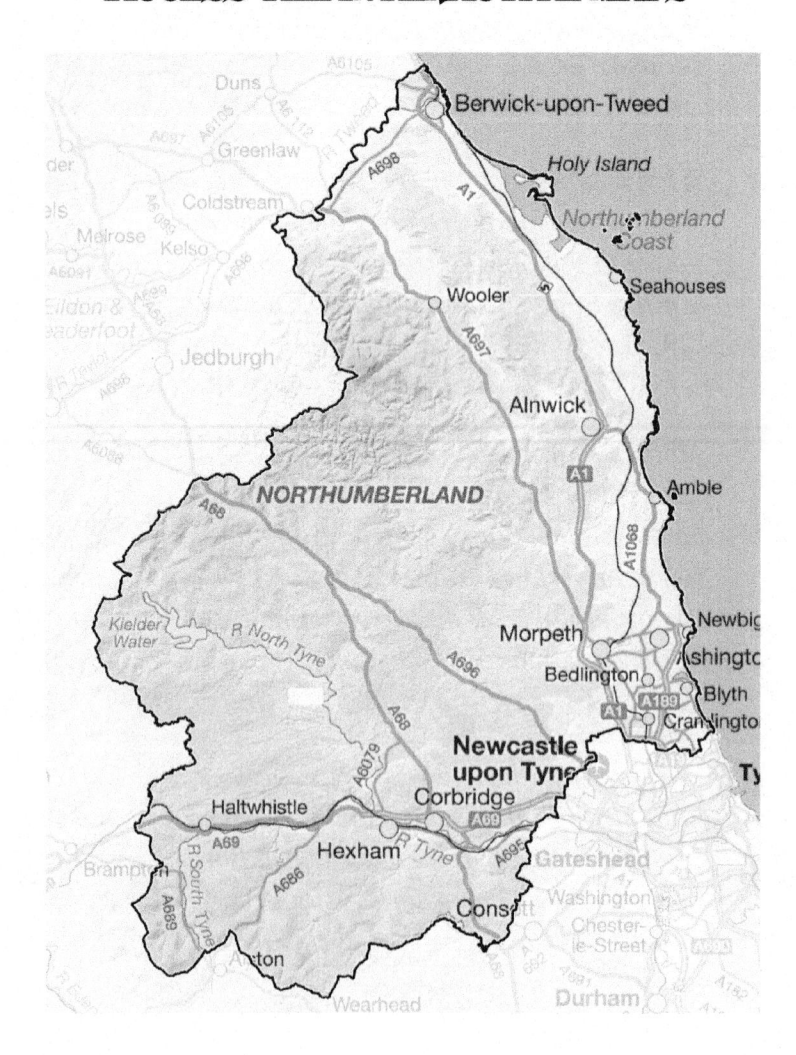

INTRODUCTION

Welcome to Northumberland

I still remember the first time I crossed into Northumberland. It wasn't a grand fanfare moment. There was no parade, no dramatic entrance—just a quiet road, rolling green hills, and a sign that read: *"Welcome to Northumberland"*. But something about that landscape made me slow down. Literally—I pulled over, got out of the car, and just stood there. The wind was sharp, the sky was impossibly wide, and in that silence, I realised I'd stumbled onto a part of England that doesn't try to impress you—it just quietly wins you over.

Why Northumberland?

So, why write a guide about this place? Why not London, or Edinburgh, or some exotic beach island where the cocktails come with paper umbrellas?

Well, Northumberland isn't like anywhere else. It doesn't shout. It doesn't show off. It doesn't even seem to care whether you notice it. And that's exactly why it's so worth your time.

This is a land of **castles older than your great-great-great-grandparents**, **beaches with more seabirds than sunbathers**, and **villages so quiet you can hear your own thoughts**. It's where you'll walk stretches of coast without seeing another soul, where ancient ruins perch dramatically on cliffs, and where even the sheep seem to have an attitude.

And did I mention the sky? No, really—the **sky here is famous**. Northumberland is home to Europe's largest area of protected dark skies. On a clear night in places like Kielder, you can see the Milky Way just hanging there like someone flung glitter across black velvet.

If you've ever wanted to feel small in the best possible way—this is where you come.

What Makes It a Hidden Gem

Let's be honest: if you asked ten people on the street where Northumberland is, at least four would guess it's somewhere near Norway. The rest might ask, "Is that part of Scotland?"

It's not. It's the **northeastern tip of England**, just before the Scottish border. And somehow, it's managed to stay a secret—tucked away behind the popularity of places like the Lake District or the Yorkshire Dales.

But here's the twist: Northumberland has **just as much natural beauty**, **way more castles**, **hardly any crowds**, and enough charm to make you rethink your favourite parts of Britain.

It's wild without being remote, ancient without being boring, and charming without trying too hard. Locals still greet you like an old friend (even when you're clearly a lost tourist), and it's one of the few places left where you can watch the tide roll in on a centuries-old causeway... and not have to queue for a selfie spot.

How to Use This Guide

This isn't your typical travel guide, stuffed with dry facts and robotic recommendations. I've walked these trails. I've gotten sunburnt at Seahouses and soaked at Alnmouth—sometimes on the same day. I've gotten lost (on purpose and by accident). And I've asked locals where to eat and what to skip. This book is the result of that journey.

Here's what you can expect:

- **Personal stories mixed with practical tips**—because knowing how to get somewhere is important, but knowing why it's worth the trip matters more.
- **Sections for different travelers**—couples, families, solo adventurers, and even folks who just want a quiet cup of tea and a castle view.
- **Hidden gems and honest insights**—including which places look great in photos but smell suspiciously like sheep up close.
- **Itineraries and seasonal tips**—so you can plan your trip with confidence, whether you're coming for a weekend or wandering for weeks.

Take this guide with you, dog-ear the pages, argue with it, follow it or ignore it—but most importantly, **use it as a gateway, not a checklist**.

Fun Facts You Didn't Know About Northumberland

Just to whet your appetite, here are a few nuggets I picked up along the way:

- Northumberland has **more castles than any other English county**. Yes, even more than those showy southern places.

- The Holy Island of Lindisfarne can **only be reached at low tide**—unless you like swimming with your luggage.
- It's the **least densely populated county in England**, which explains why you'll often share a view with only cows and clouds.
- The Sycamore Gap tree (famously featured in *Robin Hood: Prince of Thieves*) became so iconic it had its own fan club… and sadly, it made headlines again in 2023 when it was cut down. A heartbreak for many, but its legacy still stands proud along Hadrian's Wall.
- The local dialect—Geordie with a Northumbrian twist—is beautiful, musical, and occasionally impossible to translate.

That's just the beginning.

If you're the kind of traveler who likes to explore slowly, talk to strangers, wander without a plan, or find beauty in the forgotten—I think you'll fall for Northumberland the same way I did. Maybe even harder.

Now, let's begin your journey.

Where do you want to go first—castles, coastlines, or Roman roads?

CHAPTER 1: PLANNING YOUR NORTHUMBERLAND ADVENTURE

If you've ever packed a suitcase and felt the thrill of adventure rumbling in your chest, you'll understand why this chapter matters. Northumberland is beautiful, but it plays by its own rules. One minute you'll be wandering in golden sunlight past castle walls; the next, you're squinting through rain, mumbling something about buying a better coat.

Think of this chapter as your trusty travel friend—saving you from soggy socks, missed trains, and running from cows.

When to Visit (Seasons & Weather)

"What's the best time to visit Northumberland?"
I get asked this a lot. The honest answer is—it depends on what you want, and how much weather you can handle.

Spring (March to May)

Spring here is gentle. The fields start to wake up with lambs leaping around, wildflowers poke through old stone walls, and villages stretch off the winter chill. Alnwick Garden's famous cherry blossoms usually put on their show in late April to early May—well worth timing your trip.

- Expect temperatures around 6–12°C (43–54°F).
- Bring a rain jacket. It might drizzle, but that's part of the charm.

Summer (June to August)

Summer is "peak season"—though in Northumberland that still feels delightfully calm. The coastal towns come alive, pubs spill out onto the streets, and you might even spot locals risking sunburn.

- Average highs of 16–20°C (61–68°F), but there are surprise scorchers and stubborn cold snaps.
- Perfect for beach days, boat trips to see puffins, and long castle walks.

Autumn (September to November)

My personal favourite. The Cheviot Hills are blush with orange and red. Villages smell of wood smoke, and tourist numbers dwindle.

- Temperatures cool to 10–15°C (50–59°F).
- Great for stargazing, as the nights draw in and the dark skies come alive.

Winter (December to February)

If you like empty beaches, ghostly castles in frost, and a pint by a roaring pub fire, winter's your friend.

- Expect 2–6°C (36–43°F).
- Snow visits the hills, not always the coast. Short days, but atmospheric.

So pick your season—but remember, in Northumberland it's best to pack for all four in one day. Locals will tell you the weather's "changeable," which is polite code for "utterly unpredictable."

Getting There: Trains, Buses, Airports & Car Hire

By Train

Trains are the easiest way if you're coming from afar. The East Coast Main Line is a gift—smooth, scenic, and surprisingly fast.

- From **London King's Cross**, it's about 3.5 hours to Alnmouth (for Alnwick) or Berwick-upon-Tweed.
- From **Edinburgh**, just under an hour to Berwick.
- From **Newcastle**, half an hour gets you to Morpeth or Alnmouth.

I love arriving by train—watching castles and coast whiz by the window. Beats the motorway any day.

By Bus

Buses are your slower, cheaper option. They connect most towns and even small villages, though timetables can be thin on Sundays.

- Main operators: **Arriva North East** and **Go North East**.
- The **418 Coastal Route** from Alnwick to Seahouses and Bamburgh is a mini sightseeing tour in itself.

By Air

Flying in? **Newcastle International Airport** is your nearest big hub. It's linked by metro to Newcastle city centre, then by train or bus to Northumberland.

Car Hire

Honestly, if you want to explore hidden beaches, moors and castle corners, hire a car. Distances look short on a map, but lanes are winding and buses infrequent.

- Rental desks are at Newcastle Airport and in town centres.
- Tip: Always check your petrol gauge. Some villages have exactly zero fuel stations. (I found out the hard way, pushing the car into Wooler with a helpful sheep staring on.)

Getting Around: Public Transport, Driving, and Walking

Public Transport

- **Trains** zip between major stops like Berwick, Alnmouth, and Hexham.
- **Buses** cover the coast and market towns but might vanish by early evening—check last bus times, or you'll be asking the pub landlord for a bed.

Driving

Driving in Northumberland is a dream—wide views, quiet roads, the occasional medieval ruin popping up around a bend.

- Just watch out for single-track lanes. They're charming until you meet a tractor and must reverse half a mile, smiling like it's fun.

Walking & Cycling

This country was made for wandering. Public footpaths crisscross everywhere—through sheep fields, up hills, across craggy coast.

- Bring sturdy boots. Mud here is ambitious.
- Cyclists love the **Sandstone Way** or gentle trails along Hadrian's Wall.

Local Customs & Travel Etiquette

Northumbrians are famously friendly—some say the friendliest in England. But a few local tips:

- Always greet people on footpaths. Even a nod does.
- Don't climb farm gates or shortcut through fields without signs—stick to footpaths.
- In pubs, you order at the bar. Waiting for table service will make you look very lost.
- Locals have a dry humour. If someone jokes "Watch out, dragons round here," just laugh. It's tradition.

Safety Tips and Emergency Contacts

Generally, this is one of the safest counties in the UK. But a few things can catch you out:

- Always check **tide times** before crossing to Holy Island (Lindisfarne). Twice daily the causeway disappears. Many tourists have learned this lesson via cold feet—and local lifeboat crews.
- Phone signals vanish in the hills. Download offline maps.
- In a real emergency, dial **999**. For minor police help, call **101**.
- For NHS medical advice, dial **111**.

Local hospitals:

- **Wansbeck General Hospital** (Ashington)
- **Northumbria Specialist Emergency Care** (Cramlington)

Currency, Costs & Budgeting Tips

Bring **British Pounds (£)**. Most places accept cards, but small village shops or country pubs might still prefer cash.

Sample Costs (2025)

- Pub meal: £12–£20
- Coffee & cake: £5

- Castle entry: £8–£18
- Coastal boat trip to see puffins: £20–£35
- Bus rides: £2.50–£5

Budget tip: Many walks, beaches, and castle views are gloriously free. Pay for the occasional ticket—spend the savings on local ale or fresh seafood.

What to Pack: Year-Round Essentials

I've said it before, but it's worth repeating: Northumberland's weather is magical. Be ready for anything.

- Waterproof jacket (light and good quality)
- Layers (fleece, jumper, light thermal)
- Walking boots (the muddier they get, the more you belong)
- Warm hat and gloves—even in summer evenings
- Binoculars for spotting seals, puffins, or your lost hiking partner
- A small rucksack for water, snacks, and that emergency biscuit stash
- Printed maps or downloaded routes
- A phone power bank (your GPS will drain itself heroically trying to find signal)

And that's how you set yourself up for success here. Think of it as groundwork—packing your curiosity alongside your socks.

CHAPTER 2: TOP 10 MUST-SEE ATTRACTIONS

You know that moment when you stand somewhere and feel your heart do a small somersault? That's what Northumberland's best spots are all about. This chapter is my personal treasure chest—the top ten places where I've stopped, sighed, and thought, *"This alone makes the trip worth it."*

It's a glorious mix: mighty castles that look like they were designed by dragons, seaside villages that smell of salt and smoked fish, Roman walls that have stood firm for two thousand years, and nature so raw it feels almost prehistoric.

In these pages, I'll take you through:

- **Ancient fortresses like Bamburgh and Alnwick**, where history is still alive (sometimes literally—wait till I tell you about the ghost stories).
- **Dramatic coastlines**, with empty sands stretching for miles and puffins bobbing on rocks.
- **Hadrian's Wall**, where you can walk the same paths Roman soldiers once marched.
- **Tiny villages**, colourful and sleepy, perfect for lazy afternoons with tea and a slice of cake.

Each of these places is here for a reason. Not because they look good on a postcard—though they certainly do—but because they make you feel something. Awe. Joy. Sometimes just a quiet calm that settles in your bones.

And don't worry, I'll also throw in the small practical bits—like where to park, what to eat, and how not to embarrass yourself by getting stranded on a tidal island. (It happens more often than you'd think.)

How This Chapter Works

Think of this chapter as a gentle walking tour, except you can enjoy it from your armchair until you're ready to lace up your boots. Each attraction gets its own story, sprinkled with practical details:

- What makes it special?
- How do you get there?
- When's the best time to visit?
- Little tips to make your experience richer.

Bamburgh Castle: Fortress by the Sea

I've stood in front of plenty of castles in my travels, but nothing quite prepares you for your first glimpse of Bamburgh. Rising out of the dunes on the rugged Northumberland coast, it looks less like a building and more like something carved by giants — all stone and storm and legend.

My First Sight of Bamburgh

The first time I drove into Bamburgh village, I nearly ran off the road. Not from reckless driving, mind you, but because Bamburgh Castle simply **appeared out of**

nowhere. One moment, it was rolling fields and a few sheep giving me judgmental stares, the next — a colossal medieval fortress perched dramatically above the North Sea, with waves crashing at its feet.

I pulled over by a wooden fence, got out, and just stood there. It's hard to explain: there's something about seeing ancient stone towers silhouetted against a bruised grey sky, gulls wheeling around like scraps of paper, that makes the hairs on your neck stand up.

If a place could whisper, *"Imagine the stories I've seen..."* — Bamburgh would.

A Little History (But Not the Boring Kind)

Bamburgh Castle has been standing guard over this coast for over **1,400 years**. It began as the seat of the Kings of Northumbria in the 6th century, and it's been rebuilt, battered, besieged, and restored more times than most places have changed curtains.

The Normans gave it those mighty stone walls in the 11th century. In the Wars of the Roses, it was the first English castle ever defeated by artillery — a pretty big deal at the time. Then, like all grand things, it fell into ruin until the Victorian industrialist Lord Armstrong (of Cragside fame) bought it in the late 1800s and lovingly restored it.

Now it's still owned by the Armstrong family — a real lived-in castle, not just a fossil. And yes, it's open for curious wanderers like us.

Exploring the Castle

Walking up to the main gate feels like crossing into another world. The wind smells of seaweed and salt, and sometimes the roar of the ocean actually drowns out your own thoughts. Inside, you'll find:

- **The King's Hall**, with a hammer-beam roof so grand it practically echoes with the ghosts of banquets past.
- **The armoury**, filled with swords, shields, and slightly unsettling suits of armour that look like they might move if you turn your back.
- **The keep**, offering dizzying views across the North Sea. On a clear day, you can see the Farne Islands bobbing out there, like little green jewels.

Don't skip the Victorian staterooms — they're surprisingly cosy. If you're anything like me, you'll spend half the tour muttering, *"I could live here, you know,"* even though heating a place like this would probably bankrupt you.

Outside: Clifftops and Sand

Once you're done roaming the halls, take time to wander the castle grounds. Lean on a stone wall and watch the seabirds wheeling below. The castle stands on a **150-foot basalt outcrop**, which means the views over the village and along Bamburgh Beach are nothing short of spectacular.

If you walk down from the castle, you'll find one of the **most beautiful beaches in Britain** — wide, golden, often empty, stretching for miles north toward Seahouses. In summer, it's a spot for families with kites and picnics. In winter, you'll likely have it all to yourself, save for a dog chasing its tail in the surf.

When to Visit

- **Spring and summer** give you blue skies and picnics on the dunes (pack a jumper anyway).
- **Autumn** lights up the grass with gold and makes the sea look impossibly dramatic.
- **Winter storms** turn the waves into snarling beasts, and the castle feels wilder than ever.

Tip: Arrive early. Coaches roll in around late morning, and you'll want those atmospheric shots without crowds.

Little Tips That Make a Big Difference

- **Parking:** There's a large car park just beneath the castle (postcode NE69 7DF). Costs around £3–£5 for a day. The village itself has some free spots, but they fill up quickly.

- **Tickets:** Around £15 for adults (2025 price), with discounts for families and seniors. The grounds alone are worth it.
- **Food:** The Copper Kettle Tearoom in the village makes a mean crab sandwich. Or try the Lord Crewe Hotel for something heartier.
- **Dogs:** Allowed in the grounds but not inside the staterooms — though they might still appreciate the sea breeze.

A Few Quirky Extras

- Look out for the **Grace Darling Museum** just down the road. She was a lighthouse keeper's daughter who became a Victorian heroine by rowing out into a storm to save shipwrecked sailors.
- Locals say if you stand on Bamburgh beach at dusk, you might spot phantom horses galloping along the shoreline. I can't confirm — but it does add a certain thrill when the wind howls.

Why I Think It Matters

Bamburgh isn't just another castle ticked off a list. It's a place where you feel the layers of history pressing close — where Vikings once raided, kings plotted, and now families munch sandwiches on ramparts.

Standing there, with the wind tugging at your coat and the sea stretching off into forever, you understand why people have been drawn to this spot for over a thousand years.

And if you're anything like me, you'll promise yourself you'll come back — because once is never quite enough.

Alnwick Castle & Gardens: Harry Potter and More

Some places feel like fairy tales. Alnwick doesn't just feel like one — it practically **wrote the script**.

I've been to Alnwick more times than I care to count, and it still catches me off guard. One moment you're driving through rolling farmland, maybe stuck behind a tractor (a classic Northumberland traffic jam), then suddenly — **bam!** — this colossal medieval fortress rises ahead, stone towers and battlements bold against the sky.

It's so perfect it almost looks fake, like someone dropped a giant movie set into the countryside. Which, as it happens, isn't too far from the truth.

First Impressions

The first time I walked up the drive, I half expected a dragon to swoop down and circle the towers. Instead, I got an old black Labrador who trotted over, sniffed my hand, and then wandered off — apparently unimpressed.

From the outside, Alnwick Castle is all serious business: thick curtain walls, arrow slits, the kind of sturdy gatehouse that once kept rampaging Scots at bay. Inside, it's surprisingly graceful. There are sweeping lawns, ornate Italianate architecture, and even carved lions perched like slightly bored guardians.

A Place of Real Kings and Fictional Wizards

Alnwick Castle has been home to the **Percy family — the Dukes of Northumberland — for over 700 years.** That's not a typo. Seven. Hundred. Years. The current Duke and Duchess still live here when it's not teeming with curious visitors like you and me.

It's also moonlighted as one of Britain's busiest filming locations. Yes, this is **Hogwarts** from the first two Harry Potter films. Remember Harry's first flying lesson? That's on Alnwick's Outer Bailey.

But it doesn't stop at wizards. Transformers, Downton Abbey, Blackadder, even Elizabeth with Cate Blanchett — all filmed here. Sometimes you catch a gardener or tour guide with a quiet grin, clearly tickled by the castle's Hollywood fame.

Exploring the Castle

Step through the gates and you'll find a fascinating clash of styles. One moment you're walking along medieval walls thinking about knights and trebuchets, the next you're inside the State Rooms, gazing at chandeliers, silk walls, and Van Dyck portraits.

- **The State Rooms** are magnificent. Lavish doesn't quite cover it. There are tapestries, carved ceilings, and enough art to make you briefly consider reading up on your European masters.
- The library is so opulent it feels almost rude to breathe. (Try not to knock over anything priceless. The Duke might not appreciate it.)
- **The Castle Courtyard** often has medieval reenactors, archery, or broomstick training for kids (and adults who still secretly want to be wizards).

Little tip: Ask the guides questions. They're a goldmine of cheeky stories — like which bedrooms are apparently haunted, or what weird demands film crews have made.

The Alnwick Garden: Not Just a Pretty Face

Next door sits **The Alnwick Garden**, a masterpiece of modern garden design. It was dreamt up by the Duchess of Northumberland, who didn't just want roses and polite hedges. She wanted something that would surprise people — and maybe even scare them a little.

- There's the **Grand Cascade**, a tumbling series of fountains that look like something out of Versailles (on a slightly rainier budget).
- The **Poison Garden** is a personal favourite. Behind big black gates, guides lead you through beds of deadly plants while telling slightly alarming stories. ("Yes, that one can stop your heart in seconds. Moving on!")

- The **Treehouse Restaurant** is one of the largest wooden treehouses in the world, complete with rope bridges and a crackling log fire. Eating fish pie up in the trees is an oddly magical experience.

When to Visit

- **Summer:** The gardens are at their lushest. Book tickets ahead for weekends — it's popular.
- **Spring:** Cherry blossoms explode into colour in April and May.
- **Autumn:** The castle and gardens glow gold. Fewer crowds, more atmosphere.
- **Winter:** The gardens host light trails and illuminations that turn it all into a sparkling wonderland.

Practical Details

- **Tickets:** For 2025, expect to pay around £20 for castle entry, £16 for the gardens — or about £35 combined. Book online for small savings and guaranteed slots.
- **Parking:** Big pay-and-display car park on the edge of town (NE66 1YU). Easy 5-minute stroll to the gates. Costs about £4–£5 for the day.
- **Food:** The castle has a café, but for something special, try lunch or tea in the Treehouse. Book ahead, especially in summer.

- **Shopping:** The garden shop is dangerously tempting — local gins, chutneys, garden gear. I once walked out with a trowel I absolutely did not need.

A Few Personal Tips

- If you're travelling with kids (or playful adults), definitely do the broomstick training sessions on the castle lawn. Watching grown men trying to levitate never gets old.
- The Poison Garden is guided entry only. Tours go every 20 minutes — worth waiting for.
- Stay till near closing time if you can. The crowds thin out, and you might just get the Outer Bailey almost to yourself, with the sun setting over the towers. It's quite something.

Why Alnwick Sticks With You

It's easy to think Alnwick's magic is mostly tied to its fame — all that Harry Potter dust still floating in the air. But it's more than that.

Standing there, with centuries pressing close on all sides, fountains leaping behind you, and maybe a kestrel gliding overhead, you realise this isn't just a place that was built — it's a place that's still alive. Still lived in. Still loved.

I left with my pockets full of ticket stubs and a camera roll packed with slightly wonky photos (the cobbles are murder on steady hands). But more than that, I left promising myself I'd come back — because Alnwick never tells you all its secrets at once.

Hadrian's Wall & Sycamore Gap: Walking With Romans

If you ever want to feel deliciously small — in that way that reminds you the world is wide, old, and full of stories bigger than your own — stand on Hadrian's Wall.

Stretching roughly **73 miles** from coast to coast, this stone ribbon winds across rolling hills and quiet sheep fields, cutting through the landscape like a scar left by ancient ambition. It was built by order of the Roman Emperor Hadrian around **AD 122**, meant to keep the wild northern tribes out of Roman Britain. (Or depending on which historian you believe, to keep the Roman soldiers busy and away from causing mischief.)

My First Time on the Wall

I'll confess: the first time I walked on Hadrian's Wall, I didn't expect much. I thought, *"It's just an old wall. How impressive can it be?"*

Then I came up over a rise near Housesteads Fort and there it was — stretching off into the horizon, climbing a green ridge, then diving down into a dip and up again like a stone roller coaster.

Suddenly, 1,900 years fell away. I could almost hear the clink of legionnaire armour, the low Latin chatter, the lonely sentry stamping his feet to keep warm. It's haunting, but quietly. The kind of haunting that fills you up rather than frightens you.

Hiking Along the Wall

Where to Start?

The best bits are in **Northumberland National Park**, roughly the central section of the Wall. Here, the wall is most intact and the landscape wildest — big skies, sweeping views, fewer crowds.

Most people choose between:

- **Housesteads Roman Fort:** One of the best-preserved Roman forts. You can still see the barracks, granaries, and even the old latrines.
- **Chesters Roman Fort:** Near Chollerford, it has elegant ruins and a small museum with Roman altars and jewellery.
- **Steel Rigg to Sycamore Gap:** Possibly the most famous short walk.

I personally love parking at **Steel Rigg** and doing the circular hike past **Sycamore Gap** (that iconic lone tree), then looping back. It's around **2–3 miles**, moderate difficulty — lots of ups and downs, so your knees will have opinions later.

Sycamore Gap: That Famous Tree

Ah, **Sycamore Gap**. Even if you think you don't know it, you probably do. It's the most photographed tree in

England — a solitary sycamore nestled in a dramatic dip along the Wall.

It starred in *Robin Hood: Prince of Thieves* with Kevin Costner (though don't try to follow Robin's sprint to Nottingham; your legs aren't that long).

Standing there feels oddly moving. The tree seems to huddle protectively in the hollow, framed by stone ramparts and endless sky. It's a place that makes people whisper without knowing why.

A Bittersweet Update

In late **2023**, the tree was tragically cut down in an act of vandalism that left the whole country grieving. But the site hasn't lost its power. The stump remains, new shoots are already sprouting, and people still come — to mourn, to marvel, and to stand quietly with their own thoughts.

Local groups plan to help it regenerate or plant a new sycamore from its seeds. If that's not a hopeful metaphor, I don't know what is.

Best Times to Visit

- **Spring & Autumn:** The air is crisp, the hills blaze with either fresh green or rusty gold, and there are fewer walkers.

- **Summer:** Longer days make for glorious evening hikes. Bring water — the sun can still surprise you here.
- **Winter:** Stark, raw beauty. You'll need sturdy boots, layers, and possibly a hip flask of something warming.

Practical Bits

- **Parking:** Steel Rigg (NE47 7AN) is best for Sycamore Gap. It's pay-and-display, around £3–£5.
- **Facilities:** Basic looks at Steel Rigg. For real tea and cakes, stop at the Twice Brewed Inn nearby — perfect for muddy boots and weary legs.
- **Footing:** The path is uneven, with rocky steps and muddy patches. Decent walking boots are non-negotiable.

A Few Tips to Make It Special

- **Slow down.** You'll see folks racing through with fitness watches beeping. Ignore them. This is a place for lingering.
- **Look out for Roman graffiti.** Soldiers carved names and cheeky doodles into stones that still survive.
- **Stay for sunset.** The Wall catches the last light beautifully, casting long shadows over the hills.

Why I Keep Coming Back

I've walked along Hadrian's Wall in blustery rain, under blazing sun, and once during a light snow that turned the hills to sugar. Each time it felt new. Each time, I left with a deeper sense of how tiny — and somehow more precious — our stories are against the sweep of time.

It's the sort of place that makes you tuck your hands into your pockets, breathe deep, and think about all the footsteps that came before yours — Roman sandals, medieval traders, Victorian picnickers, and now your own slightly squeaky boots.

Holy Island of Lindisfarne: Tides and Tranquility

There are places in the world that feel close to the veil — like if you stand quietly enough, the past might lean in and whisper to you. Holy Island of Lindisfarne is one of them.

I've lost count of how many times I've visited, but each arrival still feels like stepping into a hushed secret. It's a tiny tidal island just off Northumberland's coast, linked to the mainland by a causeway that's only passable at low tide. Twice a day, the North Sea rolls in and cuts Lindisfarne off from the rest of the world. The island becomes an island again — private, silent, and utterly magical.

Arriving by Tide

Driving across the causeway is its own little adventure. The road unfurls ahead, flanked by nothing but mudflats and glinting water. It feels almost reckless, venturing out on a narrow strip with the sea biding its time on either side.

Pro tip: Check the tide tables religiously. Every year, some unfortunate soul tries to beat the clock, only to get stuck halfway, water lapping at their doors, waiting sheepishly for the coastguard. Locals will have a good-natured chuckle at your expense. (Though you'll be less amused by the rescue bill.)

A Place of Saints and Sagas

Holy Island's spiritual pull is old — older than England itself. Back in **AD 635**, Irish monk **St. Aidan** established a monastery here, which became a beacon of Christianity across Anglo-Saxon England. It was from Lindisfarne that missionaries spread north, shaping the spiritual map of Britain.

Then came **793 AD**, when Viking longships sliced across the horizon. They stormed the monastery in what's often marked as the start of the Viking Age. You can still sense it here: an island on the edge of things, vulnerable yet enduring.

Exploring Lindisfarne Castle

Perhaps the most striking sight is **Lindisfarne Castle**, perched dramatically atop a rocky crag at the island's southern tip. It's a compact, slightly stern-looking fortress, originally built in the 1500s. In the early 1900s, it was transformed into an elegant private home by architect **Sir Edwin Lutyens**, who gave it warm interiors and clever nooks.

Inside, it's surprisingly homely, with roaring fires, intimate rooms, and windows framing endless views of sea and sky. I've stood there by the small fireplace, imagining stormy nights with waves battering the rocks below — it's the sort of place that invites long stories and longer silences.

The Ruined Priory

In the heart of the village lie the evocative remains of **Lindisfarne Priory**. Weathered stone arches rise against the sky, where monks once chanted and illuminated manuscripts by candlelight.

The **Lindisfarne Gospels**, a masterpiece of medieval art, were created here — a breathtaking blend of Celtic, Anglo-Saxon, and Christian imagery. (They're now housed safely in the British Library, but you can almost feel their ghost here.)

Wander slowly among the ruins. Let your imagination fill in the missing roofs and painted walls. It's not hard to picture the quiet industry of monks or hear the echo of their footsteps on the cloister stones.

Wildlife and Walking

When the day trippers ebb away with the tide, Lindisfarne becomes truly special. You might have the windswept dunes all to yourself, or watch seals bobbing in the shallows. In spring and autumn, thousands of birds stop here on their migratory journeys, turning mudflats and salt marsh into bustling airports of feathers and calls.

There's a circular walk around the island, about **3.5 miles**, taking in sandy beaches, lime kilns, and views back toward Bamburgh on a clear day. It's flat, peaceful, and gives you plenty of excuses to pause and breathe.

When to Visit

- **Spring and Autumn:** Fewer visitors, plenty of birds, and the island feels closer to how it must have been centuries ago.
- **Summer:** The village bustles, ice cream shops thrive, and the gardens around the castle bloom.
- **Winter:** Stark, raw, often empty — the sea grey and moody. You'll understand why monks found this a place for contemplation.

Practical Notes

- **Tide Times:** Absolutely critical. Tide charts are posted everywhere, but check online (try the Northumberland County Council's site). The sea waits for no one.
- **Parking:** There's a large car park as you enter the village. No vehicles are allowed further in without a permit.
- **Tickets:** The castle is managed by the National Trust, around £9–£12 entry. The priory is under English Heritage, about £7–£9. Combination tickets can save you a bit.
- **Food:** Cosy cafés and pubs serve crab sandwiches, scones, and local ale. Try the **Ship Inn** or **Pilgrims Coffee House** (they roast their own beans).
- **Souvenirs:** Look for local mead. Monks brewed it here for centuries, and while today's versions

are more tourist-friendly, they still pack a warming punch.

Why Holy Island Stays With You

There's a hush on Lindisfarne you don't often find. Even with tourists about, it feels suspended between worlds — a place that remembers things long after the rest of us have forgotten.

I've walked here at sunset, when the last light spills gold across the mudflats, and felt oddly certain the monks were still somewhere close, just beyond sight.

When you drive back across the causeway as the tide starts its slow return, there's always a little tug of the heart — like leaving behind something precious you can't quite explain.

Dunstanburgh Castle Coastal Walk: Ruins and Rolling Waves

Some castles make a grand entrance — standing tall by the road, flags fluttering, gift shop at the ready. **Dunstanburgh Castle** is different. To meet it properly, you have to earn it.

This fortress refuses to be easy. It sits perched on a lonely headland between the fishing village of **Craster** and the golden sweep of **Embleton Bay**, only reachable by foot. And that's exactly why I love it. It feels like a small pilgrimage — one where each gust of sea wind scrubs your mind clean.

Setting Off from Craster

I usually start in **Craster**, a tiny village that smells wonderfully of smoked fish and salt. It's famous for its kippers — smoked right there at **Robson's smokehouse**, which has been curing herrings for over a century. If you arrive early, you might see kipper-laden trays being carried into the brick kilns.

From the car park (NE66 3TW, a few pounds for the day), it's an easy amble past stout stone cottages down to the harbour. The walk to Dunstanburgh starts at the edge of the village, through a wooden gate that opens onto rolling pasture — the North Sea immediately glittering on your left.

The Walk: Simplicity Itself

It's about **1.3 miles (2 km)** from Craster to the castle, hugging the coast the whole way. You follow a grassy track with sheep grazing lazily on one side, the restless sea on the other. Depending on the weather, the sky can be a blistering blue or a bruised, thundery grey that makes the ruins look even more gothic.

I've done this walk in every season — in summer sun, in stinging sideways rain, even once in a snow flurry that startled both me and the local sheep. Each time feels like a different story.

First Glimpse of the Castle

As you round a slight headland, **Dunstanburgh Castle** finally appears — stark and jagged against the horizon. Its towers look half-crumbled, half-defiant, like they're shrugging off the centuries.

Built in the early **1300s by Thomas, Earl of Lancaster**, it was meant to be both fortress and grand statement — a sort of "look at me" to rival the king's power. It saw its share of medieval drama and sieges, then slipped into romantic ruin.

There's something beautifully melancholy about it. It doesn't stand neatly preserved, it broods. Perched on its black whinstone cliff, waves crashing below, it feels like a place that remembers storms and battles long after we've gone.

Exploring the Ruins

For a small fee (around £6, English Heritage), you can wander inside. There's no museum clutter here — just skeletal walls, towering gatehouses, and gaps that frame the sea like paintings.

Climb up the old ramparts. The wind usually roars through these stones, and gulls wheel overhead, squawking as if they own the place. Stand there a while and look north to **Bamburgh Castle**, or south to the pale curve of Embleton Bay. You'll feel both tiny and oddly triumphant, like you've stepped into your own windswept epic.

Carrying On to Embleton Bay

If your legs are game, keep walking past the castle to **Embleton Bay**. It's one of Northumberland's loveliest beaches — wide, soft, and surprisingly empty. Even on a sunny day, you might only share it with dog walkers and brave swimmers.

Here, the castle stands back in the distance, looking more like a myth than a building. I once sat here with a flask of tea, toes buried in the cool sand, watching Dunstanburgh turn pink in the evening light. A better seat for a sunset is hard to imagine.

When to Go

- **Spring and early summer:** Wildflowers splash the headlands with colour — yellow gorse, pink thrift, purple orchids.
- **Autumn:** The light turns mellow, birds gather in flocks, and there's a rich smell of earth and salt.
- **Winter:** Fewer people, moodier skies. You'll need a hat that won't blow off, and possibly a strong sense of humour.

Practical Notes

- **Parking:** Use Craster's main car park. Avoid driving further into the village — it's tight, and local residents (quite fairly) value their peace.
- **Footwear:** The path is grassy and often muddy. Decent shoes or boots spare you soggy socks.
- **Food:** Grab smoked salmon or kippers from Robson's to take home. Or pop into the **Jolly Fisherman pub**, which does hearty pies and local ales with a view of the harbour.
- **Facilities:** Toilets by the car park. Once you're on the path, it's just you, the sheep, and the sea.

Why It Matters

Walking to Dunstanburgh is as much about the journey as the destination. It forces you to slow down, to feel the wind in your hair, to watch the play of light on the water. By the time you stand under the castle walls, you've earned it — and it feels all the more extraordinary.

And when you turn back toward Craster, the castle fading behind you, chances are you'll be already planning when to come again. I always do.

Farne Islands: Puffins, Seals & Boat Trips

If you ever want to be reminded just how wonderfully chaotic nature can be — and how small you are in the grand pecking order of things — take a boat trip to the **Farne Islands**.

Every time I go, it's the same. The boat cuts away from Seahouses harbour, engines chugging, gulls wheeling behind us hoping for a snack, and I get that small thrill: we're leaving the safe land for a scatter of rocky isles that feel like they belong more to the wild than to us.

Setting Sail from Seahouses

It all starts in **Seahouses**, a lively little harbour town where fishing boats sit shoulder to shoulder with puffin-painted tour boats. The smell here is always a mix of salt, diesel, and fresh fish — the sort of honest seaside scent that sticks to your coat.

Boat trips leave from the harbour every half hour or so in summer, depending on the weather. A quick tip: book ahead if it's peak season. And bring a hat you can tie down — otherwise the wind will have it halfway to Norway before you can say "puffin."

Out on the Water

Once you're out of the harbour, the coastline quickly becomes a postcard. Bamburgh Castle looms grandly to the south, sand dunes roll like sleepy lions, and then the Farne Islands start to appear ahead — low, rocky outcrops crusted with white (from guano, truth be told, but let's keep it poetic).

The boat slows as it weaves between the isles. Depending on your trip, you might land on one (Inner Farne and Staple Island are most common) or do a full cruise around the archipelago.

Meeting the Puffins

The puffins are undoubtedly the little celebrities here. From May to late July, thousands of them flap back to nest in burrows across the islands.

I still remember the first time I saw one up close: bright orange feet planted comically wide, beak stuffed with tiny silver sand eels, looking utterly pleased with itself. They totter about like slightly tipsy gentlemen, often pausing to stare back at you with equal curiosity.

Get ready for the racket. Alongside puffins, there are guillemots, razorbills, kittiwakes, and Arctic terns that aren't shy about telling you (loudly) if you're too close to their nest. The noise is almost joyful — like a bustling market square, but for feathers.

Grey Seals: The Other Stars

Then there are the **grey seals**, which loll on the rocks like oversized, whiskered sausages. They barely open an eye as your boat putters by. In autumn, you'll see pups, pale and fluffy, blinking up at the world with solemn black eyes.

Sometimes the seals slip into the water and pop up near the boat, following you like curious submarines. I swear they grin — though perhaps that's just wishful thinking on my part.

Landing on the Islands

If your trip includes landing (check ahead — not all do), you'll step out onto boardwalks that crisscross the rough ground. Rangers keep an eye on visitors and are always happy to answer questions.

On **Inner Farne**, you might find yourself ducking as Arctic terns dive-bomb your hat — they're only protecting their chicks, but it adds a dramatic flourish. (The island provides sticks to wave above your head — it sounds daft but works a treat.)

When to Visit

- **May to July:** Puffin season — truly spectacular.
- **September to November:** Seal pupping season.
- **Outside these times:** Still a rugged delight, with fewer crowds and plenty of birds overwintering.

Practical Notes

- **Cost:** Expect to pay around **£20–£30 per adult** for a standard boat trip, a bit more for longer or landing tours. Kids often go half price.
- **Dress warmly.** Even on sunny days, the sea wind has teeth. Layers, waterproofs, and something to keep your ears warm are wise.
- **Facilities:** Boats generally don't have loos, and the islands' facilities are basic at best — go before you sail.
- **Food:** Seahouses are your best bet. Grab fish and chips (Neptune Fish Restaurant is a local staple) before or after. Watch out for sneaky gulls — they're expert muggers.

Why the Farnes Stay With You

I've been out to the Farnes on flat-calm days where the sea looks like green glass, and on rough days where the boat smacks down so hard the spray makes you squeal. Each trip feels fresh.

It's the sheer aliveness of the place. Standing there, wind tugging at your coat, puffins bustling about their business, seals draped on rocks like exhausted aristocrats — you're reminded the world runs on its own glorious terms, with or without us.

And when the boat finally noses back into Seahouses harbour, engine easing down, you feel a little different. Like you've left part of your ordinary worries bobbing somewhere out there among the waves.

Craster Village & Kippers: A Taste of the Sea

I have a soft spot for Craster. It's not flashy, not showy — just an old fishing village that seems perfectly content to let the big castles and wide beaches nearby take all the dramatic glory. Craster is about quiet character, the smell of the sea, and, most importantly, the best smoked fish you'll ever taste.

Arriving in Craster

Whenever I come into Craster, it feels like slipping into somewhere unhurried. The road drops gently down past rolling fields (often full of sheep with that faintly scandalised look they give passing cars), then suddenly you're by a tiny harbour, with sturdy old boats moored to thick ropes.

There's usually a breeze, stiff enough to flap your coat open and set gulls shrieking overhead. The cottages are built from grey stone, their walls patched with lichen and salt marks. It's honest architecture — nothing fancy, just built to stand up to centuries of storms.

The Harbour: Heart of the Village

The harbour itself is small, almost pocket-sized, built in the 1800s to serve the local quarry. Now, it's mostly fishing and pleasure boats, plus a handful of photographers trying to catch that perfect reflection shot.

I once sat on a bench here for nearly an hour, just watching the tide creep in, the boats rise ever so slightly, and locals wander by with dogs who all seem to have important business to sniff out.

The Famous Kippers

But let's be honest — the real reason most people come to Craster is the kippers. And who could blame them?

Right by the harbour sits **L. Robson & Sons Smokehouse**, an institution that's been curing herring since the late 1800s. You'll usually smell it before you see it: that deep, mouthwatering scent of wood smoke and oily fish. They use traditional oak smoking methods, turning plump North Sea herrings into Craster kippers — rich, golden, and shimmering slightly like bronze.

I'll warn you: once you've had a Craster kipper, the ones in plastic supermarket packs back home will taste like damp cardboard.

Trying Them for Yourself

Most local pubs and tearooms serve kippers for breakfast or lunch — grilled and split, often with a hunk of bread to mop up the juices. A slightly messy affair, but that's half the fun.

One morning I ordered kippers at the **Jolly Fisherman**, a cosy pub overlooking the harbour, and the waitress gave me a cheeky grin.
"First time with proper kippers?" she asked.
I admitted it was.
"Just mind your shirt. They bite back."

She wasn't wrong. By the end, I had a few tiny splatters of golden oil on my collar and absolutely no regrets.

More Than Just Fish

If you can tear yourself away from the smell of smoking herring, Craster is also the perfect jumping-off point for walks along the coast. The most popular is the **1.3 mile stroll to Dunstanburgh Castle**, with the sea on one side and meadows on the other. But you can also head the opposite direction toward Cullernose Point, where dramatic cliffs plunge straight into frothy waves.

Practical Tips

- **Parking:** There's a pay-and-display lot as you come into the village (NE66 3TW). It's a short stroll down to the harbour — don't try to squeeze into tiny village streets.
- **Shops:** Robson's has a shop next to the smokehouse, so you can buy kippers to take home (they'll even vacuum-pack them).
- **Food:** The **Jolly Fisherman** is beloved for a reason — excellent crab sandwiches, local ales, and that glorious view over the harbour.
- **Toilets:** Public loos by the car park. Always worth a quick visit before setting off on coastal walks.

Why Craster Stays With You

Craster isn't grand. It won't wow you like Bamburgh or make you feel ghostly whispers like Lindisfarne. What it does is simpler and somehow just as precious: it lets you slow down.

You sit on a bench by the harbour, hands still smelling faintly of smoked fish, watch the boats bob in the tide, and think, "This is enough." And for that hour, it absolutely is.

Northumberland National Park: The Wild Heart

If you want to feel Northumberland breathe — to hear it sigh through the grass and ripple across ancient hills — come to **Northumberland National Park**.

It stretches from the middle of the county all the way up to the Scottish border, a vast sweep of moor, heather, rugged hills, and lonely valleys. You could walk here all day and never see another soul, except maybe a startled sheep or a curlew calling somewhere out of sight.

This is England's **least visited national park**, which is exactly why it's so magical. No queues, no theme cafés, no crowds jostling for selfies — just raw, unspoiled nature that goes on and on.

My First Time in the Park

I still remember the first time I drove into the park, heading north out of Rothbury. The road twisted higher, hedges gave way to rough stone walls, then suddenly the land opened up into a rolling, restless sea of green and brown.

I pulled over at a layby near **Simonside**, got out, and just stood there. The only sound was the wind rushing over the heather. For a moment, it felt like I'd stumbled off the map entirely — into a wilder, older England.

Highlights You Shouldn't Miss

Simonside Hills

Near Rothbury, these hills rise like dark green shoulders, streaked with rocky outcrops. A hike up here is short but packs a punch. From the top, you can see all the way to the Cheviots in the north, and on a clear day, out toward the coast.

Legend has it these hills are haunted by **duergar** — mischievous dwarves who lead travellers astray with dancing lights. I can't say I saw any, but I did nearly twist an ankle on the rocky path, which might count as mischief.

The Cheviot and the College Valley

Further north are the **Cheviot Hills**, rolling and sheep-dotted, stretching right across into Scotland. The highest, simply called **The Cheviot**, stands at 815 metres. It's no Everest, but the climb still leaves you breathless, rewarded with views so wide your eyes don't know where to stop.

Nearby lies the remote **College Valley**, a peaceful, protected area that feels utterly cut off. It's one of my favourite spots for long, slow walks where the only company is skylarks and the occasional startled rabbit.

Hadrian's Wall in the Park

The central section of **Hadrian's Wall** runs right through the park, often crossing some of its wildest terrain. Places like **Steel Rigg** and **Housesteads Fort** aren't just about Roman stones; they're about standing with history on a windswept ridge, watching the land ripple away under big, dramatic skies.

Nature in Abundance

Northumberland National Park is full of wildlife if you pause long enough to look. You might see:

- **Curlews and lapwings**, calling with that eerie, fluting song.
- **Red squirrels**, still hanging on here where greys have yet to bully them out.

- In summer, the heather turns whole hillsides a soft, startling purple, buzzing with bees.

At night, it's one of the best places in England for **stargazing**. The park is part of **Northumberland International Dark Sky Park**, the largest area of protected dark skies in Europe. I once lay flat on my back by a dry stone wall near Bellingham, counting shooting stars until my neck ached.

When to Visit

- **Spring:** Lambs tumble over the hills, birds start their noisy courtships, and the air feels newly scrubbed.
- **Summer:** Best for long hikes and that purple heather spectacle.
- **Autumn:** Rusty bracken and gold-flecked trees. Bring a thermos.
- **Winter:** Snow dusts the hills; it's cold, empty, and quietly spectacular. You'll want sturdy boots and probably a backup flask of something stronger than tea.

Practical Bits

- **Getting there:** The park covers a huge area with no single entrance. Most visitors drive in from Rothbury, Alnwick, or up from Hexham.
- **Facilities:** Sparse. This is part of the charm — pack snacks, water, and a sense of independence.

- **Maps:** Pick up an **OS Explorer map** for the best experience. GPS can be flaky. There's real delight in finding your own way.

Why This Place Grabs Your Heart

There's something about Northumberland National Park that feels honest. It's not prettified or fussed over. The fences lean, the sheep are suspicious, and the winds have a way of rummaging right through your thoughts.

I've stood alone on a ridge here, coat zipped to my nose, and felt that rare, wonderful kind of small that reminds you the world is vast and your troubles are not quite as heavy as they seemed.

It's the wild heart of Northumberland — and if you let it, it'll become a little bit of your own heart too.

Kielder Water & Observatory: Dark Sky Magic

If there's anywhere in England that can make you feel like you've stumbled onto another planet, it's **Kielder**. The first time I drove out here, winding along empty roads through towering pines, it felt like I was being swallowed up by a green, breathing giant. Then the trees parted and there it was — **Kielder Water**, the largest man-made lake in Northern Europe, spread out like a gleaming coin tossed into the middle of all that forest.

The Call of the Water

Kielder Water is huge — **27 miles of shoreline**, to be precise. It was built in the 1970s as a reservoir, flooding an entire valley (if you ask old locals, you'll hear bittersweet stories about farms and cottages now resting under 50 feet of water).

Today, it's a vast playground. Sailboats carve slow arcs across the surface, cyclists spin along the 26-mile Lakeside Way, fishermen stand hip-deep by the shore hoping for trout, and kids squeal on zip lines at **Leaplish Waterside Park**.

I once hired a bike on a whim, planning to "just do a short bit." Three hours later, legs aching, still nowhere near finishing the loop, I was laughing like an idiot. It's that kind of place — it expands your day without you noticing.

Kielder Forest: England's Green Cathedral

Surrounding the lake is **Kielder Forest**, the largest man-made forest in England, with over **150 million trees**. It's a deep, mossy world of towering spruce and pine, woodpeckers drumming, and sudden clearings where deer might be watching you watch them.

Some bits feel almost primeval. I once stepped off the main track for a wander and found myself in a patch where the trees were so thick it felt like dusk at midday. You half expect to see antlers slip between the trunks or hear a long-lost Saxon hunter crunching through the leaves.

Kielder Observatory: Stars Like You've Never Seen

But the real magic of Kielder comes after the sun dips behind those endless hills. Because here, far from city lights, is one of the **darkest places in Europe** — part of the **Northumberland International Dark Sky Park**.

Perched high on a hill is **Kielder Observatory**, an architectural marvel that looks like something out of a science fiction film — all timber angles and wide decks pointed at infinity.

I went up for an evening event once, clutching a flask of tea and layered up like an arctic explorer. The astronomers were full of infectious wonder, pointing out constellations with laser pens, reeling off facts that made my head spin.

Through their telescopes I saw the craters of the moon so clearly it felt like cheating. Then they swung it to Saturn — and there it was, rings and all, hanging in the blackness. I think I actually gasped.

Why It Stays With You

There's something profound about standing under that dark dome of sky. It's like the universe is quietly saying, *"Look how big I am — and you're part of it."*

I ended that night flat on my back on one of their outdoor benches, eyes darting from star to star, trying to catch shooting meteors. It was freezing, my tea had long gone cold, but I couldn't have felt warmer.

Practical Tips

- **Visiting the Observatory:** You have to **book in advance** — popular nights sell out weeks ahead, especially meteor showers. Check their calendar for family nights, planet-watching events, or deep-space sessions.
- **Dress for the Arctic:** Even in summer, it's bitter up there. Hats, gloves, thick socks — you'll thank me.
- **Kielder village:** Tiny, with just a few places to stay or eat. Best to plan a day trip from Hexham or even Alnwick, or book a lodge by the lake.
- **Wildlife:** Keep eyes peeled — red squirrels, otters, roe deer. In summer, bats flit through the trees at dusk.

When to Go

- **Spring & Summer:** Ideal for long hikes, cycling, sailing, and catching the soft twilight.
- **Autumn:** Forests blaze gold and rust, and it's rutting season for deer — you might hear eerie bellows echoing through the trees.
- **Winter:** Stark, silent, sometimes snow-blanketed. And the longest nights for the best stargazing.

Why Kielder Is Northumberland's Secret Spell

Kielder has a way of pulling you right out of yourself. The sheer scale — of the water, the forest, the night sky — makes your everyday thoughts seem tiny.

I always leave feeling somehow reset. Like I've been quietly reminded how wide the world is, how small my worries are, and how lucky I am to be here to see any of it at all.

Warkworth Village & Castle: A Medieval Jewel on the Coquet

I have a soft spot for Warkworth. Maybe it's because it feels like a place the centuries forgot to hustle along. Or maybe it's because the first time I walked its main street — past sandstone cottages, bright flower boxes, and the occasional pub sign creaking in the wind — I half expected a knight in slightly rusty armour to come trotting by on a horse.

It's small, friendly, and cradled in a perfect loop of the **River Coquet**, like the village decided it was safer to keep the water wrapped around it for company.

Wandering the Village

The heart of Warkworth is a single street, gently curving up toward the castle on the hill. Along the way you'll pass cosy tearooms, galleries, little shops selling local crafts, and more than a few benches to sit and watch the world amble by.

I popped into **Cabosse**, a tiny chocolate shop, purely on research grounds, of course. Five minutes later I walked out with a bag of dark chocolate truffles I solemnly intended to save for later. (They made it exactly as far as the next bench.)

Warkworth Castle: Echoes of Earls

At the top of the hill stands **Warkworth Castle**, one of the most imposing fortresses in the north — and yet, curiously, never quite crowded. From the outside, its great keep rises proudly above the trees, looking every inch the home of powerful medieval earls (which it was).

Built mostly in the 14th century, this was once the stronghold of the mighty **Percy family** — the same Percys who show up all over English history books, usually sword in hand. Shakespeare even gave them a star turn in the character of **"Hotspur"** (Henry Percy), who raged through *Henry IV, Part 1* with more gusto than sense.

Exploring the Castle

Wandering the castle is a delight. There are spiral staircases to climb, grand halls to echo your footsteps in, and arrow slits framing little paintings of the countryside. Stand on the ramparts and look down at the Coquet looping around the village like a lazy silver ribbon.

My favourite bit is the great keep — part fortress, part grand home. It's surprisingly intact inside, with fireplaces, vaulted chambers, and tall windows that spill sunlight across stone floors. You can almost hear the clink of goblets and the murmur of plots being hatched over venison feasts.

A Boat to the Hermitage

But Warkworth has another secret up its sleeve — and it's downright enchanting.

Down by the river, you'll find a little wooden ferry run by a cheerful local boatman who rows visitors across to the **Hermitage**, a 14th-century chapel carved straight into the rock. It's only reachable by boat, which feels deliciously mysterious.

The Hermitage is small, cool, and eerie in the best way. A simple stone altar, weathered graves, and rough walls still bearing the marks of medieval chisels. I stood there imagining solitary monks whispering prayers to the river. Even if you're not the contemplative type, it's quietly moving.

Practical Notes

- **Parking:** There's a main car park just off the river (NE65 0UJ), with a short stroll up to the village.
- **Castle tickets:** Managed by English Heritage, around £8–£10. Audio guides are worth it for juicy stories of the Percys' squabbles.

- **Food & drink:** Try the **Masons Arms** for hearty pub meals, or **Bertram's café** for tea and decadent cakes.
- **Boat to the Hermitage:** Open from Easter to October, weather permitting, about £6. It's a lovely, gentle glide across the Coquet.

When to Visit

- **Spring & summer:** Flower baskets spill colour over cottage walls, riverside paths glow with wildflowers, and the village hums with walkers.
- **Autumn:** The trees along the Coquet turn golden, the air is crisp, and the castle feels especially atmospheric.
- **Winter:** Fewer visitors, chilly stone halls, and the sort of fog that makes you half believe ghostly earls might wander by.

Why Warkworth Captures the Heart

It's the kind of place that seeps under your skin — not through big spectacles, but through a thousand small charms. A bright painted door, the way the castle glows at sunset, the friendly nod of locals who seem genuinely pleased you've come to see their village.

And as you head back to your car, chocolate wrappers in pocket, castle towers peeking over the trees, there's a quiet certainty: you'll come back. Because places like this always leave a little mark on you, somewhere soft and stubborn.

CHAPTER 3: NORTHUMBERLAND'S ENCHANTED CASTLES

Northumberland doesn't just have castles — it practically **overflows** with them. Big dramatic fortresses, tumbledown towers, places that look like they were plucked out of a ghost story.

It's no wonder, really. For centuries, this was a land caught between England and Scotland, where neighbours were friendly but kept an eye on your cattle all the same.

In this chapter, I'll take you with me through some of my favourite castles. Each one tells a different tale, from eerie whispers to sunlit gardens. By the end, I promise you'll never look at an old stone wall quite the same way again.

Chillingham Castle: The Most Haunted in Britain

If ever a castle looked like it should be haunted, it's **Chillingham**. Set among rolling parkland, its grey walls and looming towers seem to dare the clouds to keep away.

I drove up the long winding drive feeling half thrilled, half ridiculous — as if some pale face might suddenly appear at a window.

Inside, Chillingham leans into its reputation. The place is brimming with dark wood, shadowy corners, suits of armour that look suspiciously ready to move. Guides will cheerfully tell you about the **"Blue Boy"**, who supposedly wailed through the halls until bones were found in a wall. Then there's the torture chamber — still outfitted with devices that make you cross your legs instinctively.

Yet for all its spookiness, Chillingham is oddly beautiful. There's a grand hall that fills with light, a courtyard perfect for a nervous tea, and vast gardens outside that soften all the ghosts' edges.

And then, there are the **wild white cattle** — a rare, ancient breed that roams nearby, unchanged for centuries, eyes watchful under curling horns. They look like they belong on a medieval tapestry, not the 21st century.

Practical tips:

- Open from spring to autumn, with ghost tours in summer that book up fast.
- Entry is around **£12–£15**, worth every spine-tingling penny.
- Wear sturdy shoes — old stone floors do love to trip you.

Prudhoe Castle: Off-the-Beaten Path

Most people barrel right past **Prudhoe Castle**, headed for bigger names like Bamburgh or Alnwick. Lucky for us — it means we often get the place almost to ourselves.

Tucked above the **River Tyne**, Prudhoe feels more like a sturdy old home than a grand fortress. It's been lived in, fought over, rebuilt, and generally weathered time like a champ. Unlike many Northumberland castles, it never actually fell to the Scots. I imagine it stands a little prouder because of that.

Inside, there's a modest keep, peaceful grassy baileys where children tumble about, and stout curtain walls that you can stroll atop. It's less about dramatic grandeur, more about quiet stories.

I once sat on a sun-warmed step here for nearly an hour, eating a squashed sandwich and listening to the wind rustle the trees. If any ghost appeared, it would have offered half my cheese and pickle.

Practical tips:

- Managed by English Heritage; adult tickets around **£7**.
- Bring a picnic — the grounds are wonderfully relaxed.
- A good stop on the way to Hexham or Hadrian's Wall.

Etal & Norham Castles: Border Strongholds

Further north, almost brushing Scotland's shoulder, lie **Etal** and **Norham Castles** — once fierce guardians of England's border. Today, they're glorious ruins where crows rule the ramparts.

Etal Castle sits in a pretty village of white cottages and a cosy pub (the **Black Bull**, excellent for a pint). The castle itself is modest but full of spirit, with broken towers and thick walls that once bristled with archers. You can wander freely, imagining long-ago skirmishes across the River Tweed.

Norham Castle, meanwhile, was a heavyweight in border defence. Even the mighty Scottish king James IV laid siege here. Now it's mostly walls and high, shattered keeps — but stand up there on a breezy day and you'll feel the tension that must have once crackled across these battlements.

I find both castles strangely peaceful now. The centuries have worn away the clash of swords, leaving only birdsong and the occasional bleat from sheep munching right up to the old stone.

Practical tips:

- Free or very low-cost entry, with helpful little info boards.
- Great for kids to clamber about (carefully!).
- The drive between Etal and Norham is scenic — watch for farm shops selling jams and local cheese.

Belsay Hall and Castle: Grand Estates & Gardens

Belsay is a treat — part graceful country house, part rugged medieval castle, tied together by gardens that seem spun from a fairytale.

The **Hall** is pure Regency elegance, designed in the early 1800s by its owner himself, Sir Charles Monck. It's all clean lines and graceful columns, feeling more like a Greek villa than a Northumberland manor. Inside is quite spare, which somehow makes it easier to imagine glittering dances or hushed conversations.

From the Hall, you follow a magical path through the **Quarry Garden** — a sunken world of towering rock faces, giant ferns, and twisting paths that almost demand a bit of hide-and-seek. I once startled a pair of pheasants here who were clearly having a very private conference.

Eventually you emerge at the **medieval castle**, older and rougher, its keep still climbable for sweeping views of the countryside. It's like walking from one century to another in the space of ten minutes.

Practical tips:

- Run by English Heritage; tickets around **£12**.
- The tearoom by the Hall is excellent for scones (they don't stint on the cream).

- Visit in spring for rhododendrons that look like someone's dropped pink fireworks all over the place.

Why These Castles Matter

In Northumberland, castles aren't just relics. They're part of the landscape's very bones — places that whisper stories if you pause to listen.

From ghost tales in Chillingham to the cheerful quiet of Prudhoe, from war-worn Norham and Etal to the lush daydream of Belsay, these castles remind us that history isn't just dates and battles. It's people who danced, plotted, prayed, and sometimes hid under beds when the raiders came knocking.

And if you're anything like me, by the end of this chapter you'll be peeking around every corner hoping to spot a knight — or at least a ghost with a good sense of humour.

CHAPTER 4: ROMAN BRITAIN & ANCIENT TRAILS

You can't come to Northumberland and ignore the Romans — they're everywhere. Not in togas, mind, but in the silent remains of forts, in half-buried bathhouses, in long lines of stones that once split an empire from what the Romans gloomily called **"the barbarian north."**

Hadrian's Wall is the star of the show, but there's much more here: old Roman towns, live digs where history is literally being uncovered before your eyes, and museums brimming with ancient treasures.

I've always found something wonderfully grounding about following in Roman footsteps. It's a reminder that two thousand years ago, soldiers were marching these same ridges, grumbling about the weather just like we do.

Walking Hadrian's Wall Path: Day-by-Day Guide

Walking **Hadrian's Wall Path** is one of Britain's great adventures. It's an **84-mile National Trail** that stretches coast to coast, from Wallsend in the east to Bowness-on-Solway in the west. The Northumberland stretch is its dramatic heart, where the wall climbs lonely ridges with nothing but sheep and curlews for company.

I've done it in bits and pieces (my knees prefer it that way), but here's how many tackle it over **6 days**, focusing on the most breathtaking middle sections.

Day 1: Corbridge to Chollerford (about 11 miles)

Start near Corbridge, a pretty riverside town, and walk through farmland and gentle hills. It's a good warm-up, with occasional glimpses of the old Military Road shadowing the Wall.

Day 2: Chollerford to Steel Rigg (about 13 miles)

Now the scenery turns properly epic. The Wall becomes more visible, snaking over high ground. Stop at **Chesters Roman Fort**, with its well-preserved baths by the river. By day's end, you're climbing rugged ridges toward Steel Rigg, where evening light makes the stones glow.

Day 3: Steel Rigg to Gilsland (about 9 miles)

My favourite stretch. The Wall rides the top of crags, dropping suddenly to green dips. **Sycamore Gap** pops up, made famous by *Robin Hood: Prince of Thieves*. It's hard not to stand there with hands on hips, pretending you're Kevin Costner (or glaring at tourists who do).

Day 4: Gilsland to Walton (about 8 miles)

Ruins of turrets and milecastles dot the way, plus sweeping views back to where you've come. The land starts to soften — fewer crags, more farmland.

Day 5–6: Walton to Bowness

The Wall dwindles here to earthworks, but it's peaceful, dotted with wildflowers, and there's a sense of closing a long chapter. Dip your boots in the Solway at the end and feel gloriously accomplished.

Vindolanda Fort & Live Archaeology

If you visit only **one Roman site**, let it be **Vindolanda**. About a mile south of the Wall itself, this fort and settlement have been turning up treasures for over a century.

I wandered in expecting some old stones and maybe a dusty helmet. Instead, I found one of the **most actively excavated Roman sites in Europe**, where you can watch archaeologists trowel away history in real time.

Highlights?

- The astonishing **Vindolanda Tablets** — fragile wooden postcards on which Romans scribbled everything from birthday party invites to moans about the weather.
- Deep pits revealing layers of old streets, shops, and granaries.
- Friendly guides bursting with stories, happy to show off new finds still caked in mud.

And the museum! It's packed with shoes, tools, jewellery — little things that make the Romans suddenly feel like people you might bump into at the corner shop.

Corbridge Roman Town

Down the road is **Corbridge Roman Town**, once a bustling supply base. Unlike Vindolanda's still-buried drama, here the streets are neatly laid out, easy to stroll through. You can walk along the old main road, pop your head into what were shops, granaries, and even a fountain house.

There's a good little museum too. I stood ages staring at a Roman soldier's iron helmet, wondering how many cold mornings it saw trudging up the Wall.

Corbridge village itself is charming, worth a wander for tea and local shops.

The Sill Landscape Discovery Centre

Right by **Once Brewed** (yes, that's the hamlet's actual name), sits **The Sill**, a modern visitor centre that acts as gateway to both Hadrian's Wall and Northumberland National Park.

It's beautifully done — all curved green roofs blending into the hills. Inside are interactive exhibits about the landscape, geology, and how people (Romans included) have shaped and survived in this often tough place.

They also run guided walks and nature talks. I once joined a night hike here that ended with us standing in utter darkness, the Wall a silent silhouette under a spatter of stars.

Roman Museums & History Hotspots

Beyond Vindolanda and Corbridge, there are plenty of smaller museums and sites that pull you deeper into Roman life:

- **Chesters Roman Fort** (near Chollerford): Lovely riverside spot with the best-preserved bathhouse in Britain.

- **Housesteads Fort** (near Steel Rigg): Perched dramatically with sweeping views, perfect for imagining guards scanning for marauding Picts.
- **Great North Museum** in Newcastle: Not on the Wall, but has some of the finest Roman artefacts anywhere.

Why It Matters

Walking the Wall, or poking around old forts, isn't just about ticking off historical boxes. It's about feeling connected — standing where Roman boots once crunched, reading graffiti they carved, realising they worried about cold toes and evening meals just like we do.

By the end of this chapter, you might catch yourself glancing over your shoulder for a centurion. Don't worry — it's just Northumberland working its magic again.

CHAPTER 5: COASTAL ESCAPES & SEASIDE TOWNS

If you ask me what makes Northumberland truly unforgettable, I'll probably start rambling about its coastline. It's one of those rare places that still feels wild and wide open — mile after mile of sandy beaches, tucked-away coves, dramatic castles perched on cliffs, and little villages where the smell of salt and fish and chips mingles in the air.

It's a coast that hasn't been polished up or packed out like some seaside spots down south. It's all the better for it. Here, seagulls wheel over ancient harbors, fishing boats bob gently, and you're never far from a path that leads you off into dune grass and bright horizons.

In this chapter, we'll wander through some of my favorite coastal spots — from bustling Seahouses to the painterly calm of Alnmouth. Pack a scarf (the wind here can redecorate your hairstyle in seconds), bring your appetite, and let's set off.

Seahouses: Boat Tours, Shops & Chips

If there's a single village that sums up Northumberland's seaside charm, it might be **Seahouses**. It's lively without feeling tacky, full of boat trips, chippies, and more than one seagull who'd happily snatch your lunch if you're careless.

I first came here years ago, planning to just "have a quick look." Three hours later, I'd booked a boat to the Farne Islands, eaten a frankly dangerous quantity of battered haddock, and was standing in a tiny shop buying a sweater I definitely didn't need.

Seahouses' little harbor is always buzzing — fishermen unloading lobster pots, tourists queuing for boat tours, kids leaning over to spot crabs. It's also the launch pad for trips out to the **Farne Islands**, where you can see puffins, seals, and in certain seasons, more seabirds than you thought could possibly fit on a rock.

Top tips:

- **Fish & chips:** Neptune Fish Restaurant is a personal favorite. Eat outside if you dare, but guard your chips like treasure.

- **Boat tours:** Billy Shiel's is the classic choice. Wrap up — it's cold on deck even in July.
- **Souvenirs:** Loads of little shops for nautical nicknacks, local fudge, and surprisingly stylish wool jumpers.

Beadnell Bay: Water Sports & Windswept Beauty

Just down the coast is **Beadnell**, with its sweeping crescent of golden sand that feels like it's been laid out purely for your walking pleasure.

It's popular with water sports fans — you'll see paddleboarders drifting past, kids learning to surf, and windsurfers zipping along as if pulled by invisible strings. I once tried paddleboarding here. Lasted roughly four minutes upright before the North Sea gave me a salty slap. Worth it.

But you don't need a board to love Beadnell. The dunes are perfect for lazy picnics (bring a flask, it's breezy), and if you wander along the bay toward **Newton-by-the-Sea**, you'll find yourself in a softer, quieter world of grassy tracks and hidden beach corners.

Why it's special:

- **Sunsets:** The sky seems impossibly big here, and on clear evenings the whole bay turns pink and gold.

- **Rock pools:** If you've kids — or just a curious heart — the rocks at either end of the bay hide tiny worlds of crabs, anemones, and darting fish.

Alnmouth: Colorful Cottages and Artists' Haven

Drive further south and you'll tumble into **Alnmouth**, one of the prettiest villages on the entire coast. It's a bit of a pastel dream — brightly painted houses lined up along winding streets, all set beside a wide estuary that looks like it's been painted with the softest brushes.

Alnmouth used to be a port, back when ships carried grain and fish to bigger markets. Now it's more about gentle days: gallery-hopping, sampling excellent cake, and strolling along the beach with barely a footprint ahead of you.

I've spent long mornings here just nosing around — popping into art studios, lingering over coffee at **The Village Tearooms**, and watching river boats bob lazily where the Aln meets the sea.

Good to know:

- **Art & craft:** Small galleries and shops showcase local painters and potters.
- **Walking:** A lovely coastal path connects Alnmouth to Warkworth — about 4 miles of sea views and salty air.

Berwick-upon-Tweed: Border Town with Scottish Soul

Right at the top of Northumberland, almost brushing Scotland, sits **Berwick-upon-Tweed** — a town with one foot in each country's history. Over the centuries it switched between English and Scottish hands so many times it must have given the locals whiplash.

Today it's peacefully English, but with a certain Scottish flair. The old town is wrapped in **impressive Elizabethan ramparts**, which make for a grand walk with sweeping views over the Tweed estuary and out to sea.

Berwick is also full of surprises:

- A splendid old **railway viaduct** that arches like a giant spine across the river.
- Quirky little museums detailing its days as a border fortress.
- And cosy pubs where you might hear more than a few Scottish accents still.

I love just meandering through Berwick's narrow lanes, poking into antique shops, then ending by the harbour with fish and chips as the sun sets. The light here seems to carry a softer, more northern kind of magic.

Druridge Bay Country Park

Finally, we'll pull up at **Druridge Bay**, one of those places that makes you wonder why more people don't know about it. It's a long, wild sweep of sand — seven miles of it, in fact — backed by dunes and little lakes bustling with birds.

At the heart sits **Druridge Bay Country Park**, with a tranquil lake for canoeing or just peaceful strolling. The park's visitor centre hands out maps and often has local wildlife displays (I once spent a happy hour there learning more about otters than I ever thought I needed).

It's the kind of place you come to when you want a bracing walk, followed by a flask of tea in the car while the wind tries to rock you gently to sleep.

Why This Coast Will Steal Your Heart

Northumberland's coast doesn't shout for your attention. It's not glossy or crowded. Instead, it sidles up quietly — with wind-ruffled beaches, bright little harbours, and endless skies that make you breathe deeper than you have in months.

And by the time you leave, you'll have salty lips, sand in your shoes, and that contented ache in your legs that only comes from wandering somewhere that still feels beautifully untamed.

CHAPTER 6: HIDDEN VILLAGES & MARKET TOWNS

For all Northumberland's wild coasts and brooding castles, it's often the little places that stick with me most — the villages and market towns where life still hums along at a gentler pace.

There's a unique flavour to each of them. Some have cobbled squares with farmers selling eggs out of cardboard boxes; others boast lively high streets, old theatres, riverside walks, and local galleries that surprise you with just how good they are.

In this chapter, I'll take you through a handful of my favourites. None are bustling cities. That's precisely their charm. They're places where you can slow down, chat with a shopkeeper, linger over a pint, and let Northumberland's friendly heart wrap right around you.

Rothbury: Gateway to the Cheviots

If you're headed toward the **Cheviot Hills**, chances are you'll pass through **Rothbury** — and if you've any sense, you'll stop and stay a while.

It's a classic Northumbrian market town, perched by the River Coquet, surrounded by soft green hills that seem to roll on forever. The main street is lined with stone buildings housing everything from butchers and bakers to old pubs and cheerful tearooms.

I always end up at **Tomlinson's Café**, once a Victorian workhouse, now a relaxed spot with homemade cakes and views of the river. From there, it's tempting to wander along the riverside path or nip into one of the little galleries showcasing local artists.

Rothbury also makes a perfect base for exploring the surrounding countryside. Nearby is **Cragside**, the astonishing Victorian house of inventor Lord Armstrong — the first house in the world lit by hydroelectric power. It's all fantastical rooms, quirky gadgets, and woodlands laced with walking trails.

Why you'll love Rothbury:

- Gateway to countless hikes, from gentle riverside rambles to tough climbs in the Cheviots.
- A Monday market that's delightfully old-school — fresh veg, plants, local cheeses.

- Friendly locals who might greet you as if you've lived there for years.

Wooler: A Hiker's Haven

Further into the hills lies **Wooler**, a small, sturdy town that proudly bills itself as "the gateway to Glendale and the Cheviots." It's a bit more rugged than Rothbury, with a practical air that suits its hiking boots and rucksacks crowd.

I once rolled into Wooler after a particularly wet stomp across the hills — hair plastered, socks squelching — and was still greeted with a warm grin at the local café. That's the sort of town this is.

It's not large, but it packs in outdoor shops, a fine bakery (try the Northumbrian stotties), and a few cozy pubs where you can compare blisters and plan your next route.

Nearby walks are simply glorious. **Humphrey's Hill** gives panoramic views back across the village, while longer treks lead into valleys where wild goats sometimes appear, regarding you with faint disdain.

Highlights:

- The annual **Glendale Show** — sheep, horses, crafts, and the full country fair treatment.

- Short drive to **Yeavering Bell**, an ancient hill fort that's all windswept drama and iron-age mystery.

Amble: Seafood & the Harbour Village

Swing back toward the coast and you'll find **Amble**, once mainly a fishing port, now proudly calling itself "the friendliest port in England." It's hard to disagree.

Amble has a working harbour feel — colourful fishing boats tied up alongside smart new seafood shacks. The **Harbour Village**, a neat cluster of wooden pods, sells everything from local pottery to fresh crab sandwiches. You could easily graze from one end to the other and call it lunch.

Try a stroll along the pier, watch the fishing crews sorting nets, then circle back for an ice cream (the local **Spurreli's Gelato** is famous for good reason).

Amble's also the jumping-off point for boat trips around **Coquet Island**, home to puffins, seals, and a grand lighthouse that watches over it all like a quiet old guardian.

Top reasons to visit:

- Seafood that might well have been hauled up that morning.

- A welcoming, slightly salty vibe that makes you want to linger.
- Handy base for exploring Warkworth just up the river.

Hexham: Abbey, Arts, and Riverside Charm

Step into **Hexham**, and it quickly feels a touch more refined — a handsome town set on the Tyne, with a rich medieval history balanced by a lively arts scene.

At its heart stands **Hexham Abbey**, nearly 1,300 years old. I still get goosebumps walking through the cool stone arches, imagining centuries of monks and townsfolk shuffling through these same aisles. The crypt is especially atmospheric, its old stones worn smooth by countless feet.

The town itself is full of character: cobbled streets, a pretty market square (markets still run several days a week), and independent shops selling books, antiques, and local crafts. I've lost more than a few hours rummaging through second-hand stores here.

Hexham also boasts the excellent **Queen's Hall Arts Centre**, hosting everything from theatre to live music, and riverside walks where you can breathe deep and listen to the Tyne gurgle past.

What makes Hexham shine:

- The Abbey is a must, plus the nearby **Old Gaol**, England's oldest purpose-built prison.
- Festivals and fairs that fill the streets with music, stalls, and the smell of fresh pies.
- A brilliant place to stock up on local goodies — cheeses, chutneys, artisan breads.

Haltwhistle: The Centre of Britain

Tiny **Haltwhistle** proudly calls itself "the Centre of Britain," and while various mathematicians might quibble, locals stand by it firmly. Either way, it makes for a delightful little claim to fame.

It's a quiet town on the South Tyne, with a surprisingly broad main street for its size, dotted with family-run shops and friendly cafés. What truly sets Haltwhistle apart, though, is its position right by **Hadrian's Wall Country**. It's one of the best jumping-off points for exploring the wall, with buses and trails radiating out into the hills.

A walk here is a joy — you might amble alongside flower-dotted riverbanks, or strike upward toward Roman milecastles perched dramatically on ridges. I once found myself sharing a bench with an elderly gent who gave me a thorough lecture on local history — and half his sandwich.

Why it's worth a stop:

- Close to **Housesteads** and **Vindolanda**, two top Roman sites.
- A slow, gentle pace that's hard not to fall for.
- Locals who'll likely give you a nod and a "mornin'" whether they know you or not.

Why These Towns Stay With You

What links these places isn't grandeur — it's heart. Rothbury's warm welcomes, Wooler's muddy boots and big skies, Amble's briny air, Hexham's echoes of monks, Haltwhistle's quiet pride. They're the sort of spots that seem to breathe easier, where conversations run a bit longer, and where you might find yourself thinking, "Maybe I'll just stay another day…"

And that, more than any castle or coastline, is why I keep coming back to Northumberland.

CHAPTER 7: NATURE, PARKS & STARGAZING

Northumberland isn't just a place — it's a breath of fresh air you didn't know you needed. This country has more open sky than skyline, more birdsong than car horns. It's the sort of place where you might find yourself standing in a field, grinning at nothing in particular, simply because the wind smells of heather and pine.

In this chapter, we'll wander through some of the best spots to lose (or find) yourself: sweeping national parks, forest trails, secret wildlife hides, and places where, after dark, you'll swear you're floating among the stars.

Northumberland National Park: Wildlife & Walks

Northumberland National Park stretches from Hadrian's Wall all the way up to the Scottish border, covering more than **400 square miles** of rolling hills, heather moors, and wooded valleys. It's the least populated national park in England — which means more space for you and the wildlife.

I've had days here where I barely met another soul, apart from startled rabbits and buzzards circling high overhead. It's that sort of quiet that seems to soak right into your bones.

Best ways to enjoy it?

- **Short walks:** Try the riverside paths near Ingram or gentle ambles through Breamish Valley.
- **Wildlife spotting:** Keep an eye out for curlews, red grouse, and even otters if you're lucky.
- **Spring & autumn:** My favourite times — lambs in the fields or bracken turning to burnished gold.

And if you've got kids (or just a playful streak), pop into one of the park's visitor centres, like at Walltown or The Sill, for trail maps and little nature challenges.

The Cheviot Hills: Best Trails & Panoramas

Right in the heart of the national park rise the **Cheviots**, soft, rolling hills that look inviting from afar — until you start climbing them and realise your legs have other opinions.

Still, they're worth every puff. The views from the tops are endless: wave after wave of green ridges, tiny farms nestled far below, the odd stone circle standing mysterious and patient.

Favourite hikes:

- **The Cheviot itself:** The highest point in Northumberland at **815 metres**, often shrouded in clouds like it's keeping secrets. The circular route from Harthope Valley is a leg-stretcher but incredibly satisfying.
- **Yeavering Bell:** An Iron Age hillfort that gives you 360-degree views and a real sense of ancient footsteps.

I've stood up there in whipping winds, hair standing on end, feeling both wonderfully small and oddly important — as if sharing a private nod with all the folk who climbed before me.

Kielder Forest: Bike Trails & Adventure

Now let's get truly remote. **Kielder Forest** is the largest man-made woodland in England, wrapped around **Kielder Water**, a vast reservoir that looks like a Scandinavian lake dropped in the middle of nowhere.

There's a bit of everything here:

- **Cycling:** Miles of trails, from gentle family loops to thigh-burning mountain bike routes.
- **Walking:** Lakeside circuits where you might stumble on sculptures peeking out of the trees.
- **Watersports:** Canoeing, sailing, or just skimming stones from the shore.

I once tried the mountain bike red route here. Lasted approximately three minutes before realising I was built more for cake than for jumps. Still, the slower paths are a delight — squirrels darting across your tyres, woodpeckers hammering away unseen.

Hauxley Wildlife Discovery Centre

Down on the coast, tucked near Amble, is the **Hauxley Wildlife Discovery Centre**, one of those quiet gems that most tourists zip right past. It's a restored nature reserve built on an old opencast mine — proof that if you give nature half a chance, it'll take over beautifully.

There are hides where you can spy on wading birds and waterfowl, plus friendly volunteers who'll happily show you how to identify calls. I once spent half an hour being gently scolded by a robin while trying to photograph it — turns out, birds are less obliging than castles.

Why visit?

- It's peaceful, gently educational, and perfect for an hour's stroll.
- There's a great eco café with cakes that seem to disappear mysteriously fast.

Dark Sky Discovery Sites: Where and When

Finally, when the sun dips below Northumberland's wide horizon, don't rush inside. This country is home to **some of the darkest skies in Europe**, part of the officially designated **Northumberland International Dark Sky Park**.

That means stars like you wouldn't believe — thick scatterings of the Milky Way, planets so bright they cast faint shadows, meteors streaking across the ink.

Best places for stargazing:

- **Kielder Observatory:** Join one of their evening events — powerful telescopes, expert guides, and mugs of hot chocolate to keep you warm.

- **Battlesteads near Wark:** A lovely country inn with its own observatory outback.
- **Anywhere remote:** Honestly, just pull over on a clear night, switch off your lights, and look up.

I've stood by my car many times, breath fogging, feeling small in the best way possible. It's humbling and heart-lifting all at once.

Why Nature Steals the Show Here

In Northumberland, the landscape isn't just scenery — it's the star of the story. From hilltop winds that nearly steal your hat, to woodlands that smell of moss and old secrets, to skies so dark they make your heart jump a little... it all reminds you how grand the simple world can be.

CHAPTER 8: OUTDOOR ADVENTURES FOR ALL

If you ask me, the very best way to get to know Northumberland is on your own two feet — or wheels, or even horseback. This county doesn't care if you're a seasoned hiker with calves like knotted rope, or if you just fancy a gentle ramble with frequent biscuit breaks.

There's truly something here for everyone. Whether you're travelling with excitable kids, older relatives, or you've come armed with hiking poles and ambition, you'll find miles of trails, coastal routes, bike paths, and even friendly horses just waiting to show you the wilder corners.

So grab your walking shoes (or a helmet, or paddles), and let me lead you through some of my favourite outdoor adventures.

Best Walks for Families, Seniors, and Serious Hikers

For Families:

Try the riverside paths in **Warkworth**, looping around the castle and by the Coquet. It's mostly flat, with handy benches for snack stops (essential, if your family is anything like mine).

Or wander through **Druridge Bay Country Park**, with its level lakeside trails and duck spotting.

For Seniors (or anyone fancying a gentler wander):

The lovely circuit around **Bolam Lake** is a winner — level, well-maintained, and surrounded by peaceful woodland.

The **Heritage Coast paths** also offer shorter sections that you can easily tailor — say from **Seahouses to Bamburgh**, with plenty of spots to sit and take in the sea views.

For Serious Hikers:

Hoist your daypack and tackle the **Cheviot Hills**, or stride along the craggy heart of **Hadrian's Wall Path** from Steel Rigg to Housesteads.

Expect winds strong enough to make you question your choice of hat, but views that will genuinely stop you in your tracks.

Coastal Walks with Wheelchair Access

Northumberland shines at making its beauty accessible. Many of the coastal paths have sections that are wheelchair-friendly or good for strollers.

- **Bamburgh village to the beach:** The dunes have hard-packed paths that lead to stunning views of the castle rising over the sand.
- **Seahouses harbour area:** Wide, paved paths give fantastic sea views and easy access to shops and cafés.
- **Druridge Bay Country Park:** Smooth trails circle the lake, with gentle gradients and bird hides designed for all visitors.

I've often walked these routes with older family members, or pushing a friend's pram, and never once missed out on the scenery.

Cycling Routes for All Levels

Cycling in Northumberland is bliss. Quiet country lanes, woodland tracks, and seaside promenades all combine into some of the loveliest routes in England.

For families and beginners:

- **The Coast & Castles route (National Cycle Route 1):** Choose a small section, like

Seahouses to Bamburgh. Mostly flat, with ice cream rewards at either end.
- **Kielder Lakeside Way:** A gentle loop (about 27 miles total, so pick your chunk!) with countless picnic stops and wildlife to spot.

For keen cyclists:

- Try the full stretch from **Alnwick to Berwick**, with rolling hills and sea breezes that'll keep your legs honest.
- Or tackle some of the Cheviot foothills if you fancy steeper climbs and exhilarating downhill spins.

Don't worry if you didn't pack your own bike — plenty of local hire shops offer everything from sturdy hybrids to electric e-bikes (which might save your thighs, and your dignity).

Kayaking, Surfing, and Paddleboarding

Now, if you're brave enough to get wet (and you should be — it's half the fun), Northumberland's waters await.

- **Kayaking on the Coquet River:** Gentle paddling from Warkworth lets you see herons and maybe a shy otter.
- **Surfing at Beadnell or Bamburgh:** The waves here are friendly enough for beginners,

with local schools offering lessons that end in laughter more often than wipeouts.
- **Paddleboarding on calmer days:** Try Amble harbour or even one of Kielder's quieter inlets. I promise, it's easier than it looks — and you'll only fall in once or twice before you get the hang of it.

I'll admit, I once did a very ungraceful belly flop off a paddleboard at Druridge Bay. The local gulls were highly entertained.

Horse Riding Experiences

If your idea of adventure has more hooves than handlebars, Northumberland is perfect for it. Riding here feels like stepping into a storybook — cantering along empty beaches, trotting past ancient castles, or gently plodding through green lanes and ferny woodlands.

- **Seahouses to Bamburgh beach rides:** Local stables offer escorted hacks that let you gallop (or walk, no judgment here) along wide sands with the castle in view. It's hard to beat that for drama.
- **Harthope Valley treks:** Ride through quiet upland landscapes in the shadow of the Cheviots, often with nothing but sheep for an audience.

Most stables cater to absolute beginners, so even if the last horse you sat on was a carousel, you'll be in safe hands (and probably giggling by the end).

Why Outdoor Fun Here Sticks With You

The magic of outdoor adventures in Northumberland is that they don't need to be extreme. This place is about fresh air that feels like it's scrubbing your soul clean, skies so wide they could swallow your worries, and the sort of gentle challenges that leave you grinning.

Whether it's a slow amble, a windswept cycle, or a half-soggy kayak paddle, there's always a friendly face (human or otherwise) waiting on the path ahead.

CHAPTER 9: FOOD, PUBS & LOCAL DELIGHTS

If there's one thing that surprised me most about Northumberland when I first wandered up here, it was just how good the food is. I'd expected castles, coastlines, sheep... but the hearty plates, fresh-off-the-boat seafood, crumbly cheeses and warm pies were a wonderful surprise.

And it's not just the food itself — it's *where* you enjoy it. In cosy pubs where low beams seem to hold centuries of stories, in snug tearooms that smell of scones and jam, or by the quayside with salty air and a paper cone of chips in hand.

So loosen your belt a notch and let me take you on a little tasting tour.

Best Places for Seafood: Craster, Seahouses & Amble

Northumberland's seafood is some of the best you'll find anywhere in the UK, pulled straight from the icy North Sea and onto your plate with barely a pause.

Craster:

Home of the legendary **Craster kipper** — oak-smoked herring that's so packed with flavour, it'll wake you up quicker than any coffee. Try it hot for breakfast at the **Jolly Fisherman**, where you can look out over the harbour as you tuck in.

Seahouses:

Bustling with fish and chip shops. **Neptune's** or **Lewis's** serve golden, crispy fish so fresh it practically flaps. Don't be surprised if you're dive-bombed by hopeful gulls. I once nearly lost a whole cod to an especially daring one.

Amble:

A proper working harbour, with seafood stalls selling just-caught crab, lobster and langoustine. The **Fish Shack** is a tiny wooden hut by the water that serves up knockout dishes like seafood platters and spicy crab tacos.

Top Traditional Northumbrian Dishes to Try

Food here is honest, robust, and perfect after a windswept walk.

- **Pan Haggerty:** A simple, comforting bake of potatoes, onions and cheese, sometimes with bacon. The name alone is enough to make you smile.
- **Singin' Hinnies:** Griddle scones studded with currants, the fat sizzling as they cook — hence the name, like they're singing on the pan.

- **Stotties:** A round, flat loaf that's chewy and satisfying. Locals stuff it with ham, pease pudding, or basically anything that fits.
- **Northumberland sausages:** Often spiced with herbs, best enjoyed in a soft bun with a dab of mustard.
- **Kippers, of course:** Especially if you've popped into Craster.

I once tried to recreate pan haggerty at home and managed to burn it into something that might qualify as a geological sample. Much safer — and tastier — to let the locals cook it for you.

Historic Pubs with Real Ale and Ghost Stories

No trip to Northumberland is complete without ducking into an old pub. Here the pints are often local brews, the fires crackle, and you might get more than you bargained for in the way of ghost stories.

- **The Ship Inn at Low Newton:** Right by the sea, with its own microbrewery. Perfect after a beach walk — try the crab sandwiches.
- **The Black Bull in Warkworth:** A 17th-century inn where tales swirl of ghostly regulars who never quite made it home.
- **The Rat Inn near Hexham:** Not as grim as the name suggests — it's a brilliant gastropub with clever, seasonal cooking.

I've had some of my best evenings here: a pint of Northumbrian ale, a pie that steams when you cut into it, and a local telling me about the time he swore he saw a grey lady drift past the bar.

Afternoon Tea Spots & Farm Shops

When the weather's turned moody (which Northumberland does with style), there's nothing better than ducking inside for tea and cake.

- **The Running Fox** in Felton and Longframlington is famous — huge tiered plates with sandwiches, quiches, scones, and enough sweet treats to see you through to bedtime.
- **The Alnwick Garden Treehouse:** Yes, a giant treehouse. You can take tea among the branches, feeling very much like a pampered squirrel.

And don't skip the farm shops. **Heighley Gate near Morpeth** has stacks of local cheeses and chutneys. Or stop by **North Acomb Farm Shop** for sausages that practically beg to be thrown on a breakfast plate.

Local Markets and Food Festivals

Markets here are as much a social gathering as a shopping trip. Stalls laden with fudge, game pies, smoked salmon, glistening fruit tarts. Everyone's having a chat, catching up on local gossip, and cheerfully ignoring any concept of portion control.

- **Hexham Farmers' Market:** Twice a month, with everything from honey to sourdough.
- **Alnwick Market:** Weekly, right by the old market cross.
- **Berwick Food & Beer Festival:** Held each September, where you can sample enough ale and artisan bites to warrant a nap on the town walls.

I once left with three jars of jam, a pork pie bigger than my head, and zero regrets.

Why Food Here Feels So Special

Eating in Northumberland isn't fancy. It's heartwarming, it's local, it's served by people who care. You might sit down to a meal next to muddy hikers, fancy day-trippers, and the odd dog snoozing under the table — all equally welcome.

And by the time you're rolling home, you'll have tasted more than just good cooking. You'll have had a bite of Northumberland itself: its sea air, its farmland, its friendly chatter.

CHAPTER 10: ACCOMMODATION FOR EVERY BUDGET

One of the joys of visiting Northumberland is the sheer variety of places to rest your head. You could tuck into a creaky four-poster bed in a centuries-old coaching inn, huddle up by a fire in a stone cottage by the sea, or even drift off under a canvas of stars in a luxury tent.

Here's my personal pick of the best stays, from budget-friendly beds to splurge-worthy retreats.

Historic Inns and Boutique Hotels

1. The Black Swan, Alnwick

- **Overview:** A 17th-century coaching inn turned into a charming boutique hotel, with beams, fireplaces, and seriously comfy beds.
- **Address:** 26 Narrowgate, Alnwick NE66 1JG
- **Cost:** Around £120-£160/night for a double.
- **Pro tip:** Stay midweek to avoid weekend wedding parties and snag quieter dinners.

2. Battlesteads Hotel, Wark

- **Overview:** A cosy country inn with an award-winning restaurant and its own observatory for stargazing.
- **Address:** Wark on Tyne, Hexham NE48 3LS

- **Cost:** From £130/night with breakfast.
- **Pro tip:** Book an astronomy night — telescope views plus hot chocolate under the Milky Way.

3. The Lord Crewe Hotel, Bamburgh

- **Overview:** Just steps from Bamburgh Castle, this elegant spot mixes history with modern luxury.
- **Address:** Front Street, Bamburgh NE69 7BL
- **Cost:** Around £160-£200/night.
- **Pro tip:** Ask for a castle-view room — waking up to those ramparts is pure theatre.

4. The Cookie Jar, Alnwick

- **Overview:** A boutique hotel in a converted convent. Expect plush interiors, roll-top baths, and local art.
- **Address:** 12 Bailiffgate, Alnwick NE66 1LU
- **Cost:** From £180/night.
- **Pro tip:** Try their afternoon tea even if you don't stay. It's lavish.

5. The Tankerville Arms, Wooler

- **Overview:** Historic inn on the edge of the Cheviots, perfect after long hill walks. Log fires and hearty dinners await.
- **Address:** 15 The Village, Wooler NE71 6BG
- **Cost:** Around £95-£120/night.

- **Pro tip:** Ideal for exploring Glendale and Cheviot hikes without long drives.

Budget B&Bs and Hostels

1. Alnwick Youth Hostel

- **Overview:** Housed in a former courthouse, this modern hostel has private rooms as well as dorms.
- **Address:** 34-38 Green Batt, Alnwick NE66 1TU
- **Cost:** Beds from £25, private doubles from £60.
- **Pro tip:** Great base to walk to Alnwick Castle and Gardens without paying for parking.

2. The Olde School House, Seahouses

- **Overview:** Friendly B&B in a converted Victorian school with homely breakfasts.
- **Address:** 17 North Lane, Seahouses NE68 7UQ
- **Cost:** Doubles from £75/night.
- **Pro tip:** Book ahead in summer — Seahouses fill fast due to boat trips to the Farne Islands.

3. Berwick YHA

- **Overview:** Stylish hostel right on the riverside, with views over the Tweed and bright, spacious rooms.
- **Address:** Dewar's Lane Granary, Berwick-upon-Tweed TD15 1HJ

- **Cost:** Beds from £22, privates from £65.
- **Pro tip:** Stay in Berwick for cheaper digs then a day trip by train into Edinburgh.

4. Market Cross Guest House, Belford

- **Overview:** Cosy B&B with exceptional breakfasts (try the smoked salmon).
- **Address:** 1 Market Cross Place, Belford NE70 7ND
- **Cost:** From £90/night.
- **Pro tip:** Just off the A1 — handy if you're touring by car and hopping between castles.

5. Hexham Hostel

- **Overview:** A relaxed option in this pretty market town, with simple private rooms and shared kitchen.
- **Address:** Allendale Rd, Hexham NE46 2NJ
- **Cost:** Beds from £20, private rooms from £55.
- **Pro tip:** Ideal for tackling Hadrian's Wall by day, with riverside pubs waiting when you return.

Romantic Stays and Coastal Cottages

1. Seafield Ocean Club Lodges, Seahouses

- **Overview:** Private lodges with hot tubs, steps from the dunes. Perfect sunsets.

- **Address:** Seahouses NE68 7SP
- **Cost:** From £160/night (2-night minimums).
- **Pro tip:** Book mid-autumn for golden beaches all to yourselves.

2. The Joiners Arms, Newton-by-the-Sea

- **Overview:** Quirky, luxury pub rooms with four-posters and stand-alone tubs.
- **Address:** High Newton, Alnwick NE66 3EA
- **Cost:** From £180/night.
- **Pro tip:** Splurge on dinner — the local seafood dishes are outstanding.

3. Doxford Cottages, near Embleton

- **Overview:** Beautiful stone cottages on a country estate, near quiet beaches.
- **Address:** Doxford Farm, Chathill NE67 5DW
- **Cost:** From £110/night (week-long stays often cheaper).
- **Pro tip:** Stock up on goodies at a farm shop, then spend evenings by the log burner.

4. Alnmouth Coastal Cottages

- **Overview:** A string of colourful seaside cottages in a village famed for sunsets.
- **Address:** Alnmouth NE66 2RJ
- **Cost:** Varies — around £95-£140/night.

- **Pro tip:** Check for off-season deals; winter by the coast here is stark and stunning.

5. Middlemoor Farm Holidays

- **Overview:** Chic barn conversions with panoramic rural views, great for starry nights.
- **Address:** North Charlton, Alnwick NE67 5HP
- **Cost:** From £100/night.
- **Pro tip:** Bring binoculars — you're deep in Dark Sky territory.

Family-Friendly Resorts and Holiday Parks

1. Haggerston Castle Holiday Park (Haven)

- **Overview:** Caravan park with a castle ruin, boating lake, pools, kids' shows.
- **Address:** Beal, Berwick-upon-Tweed TD15 2PA
- **Cost:** From £75/night (caravan sleeps 4-6).
- **Pro tip:** Go midweek outside school holidays for serious bargains.

2. Kielder Waterside Lodges

- **Overview:** Woodland lodges by the vast lake, packed with activities.
- **Address:** Kielder Water NE48 1BT
- **Cost:** From £140/night.
- **Pro tip:** Rent bikes on-site to explore endless forest trails together.

3. Seafield Park, Seahouses

- **Overview:** Family-run site with luxury caravans, pool, sauna — minutes from the beach.
- **Address:** Seahouses NE68 7SP
- **Cost:** From £80/night.
- **Pro tip:** Great base for Farne Island boat trips with wildlife-mad kids.

4. Berwick Holiday Park (Haven)

- **Overview:** Cliff-top site with stunning sea views, pools, sports courts.
- **Address:** Magdalene Fields, Berwick-upon-Tweed TD15 1NE
- **Cost:** From £70/night.
- **Pro tip:** Walk into Berwick for evening fish & chips by the old walls.

5. Felmoor Park Lodges

- **Overview:** Timber lodges with hot tubs, close to Alnwick and Morpeth.
- **Address:** Eshottheugh, Felton NE65 9QH
- **Cost:** From £110/night.
- **Pro tip:** Watch for local deer at dusk — they often wander through the site.

Glamping, Camping, and Eco-Lodges

1. Wild Northumbrian, near Kielder

- **Overview:** Handmade yurts, shepherd huts, and eco-cabins in total wilderness.
- **Address:** Tarset, Hexham NE48 1RT
- **Cost:** From £85/night.
- **Pro tip:** Bring a torch — it's remote, but the stargazing is unbeatable.

2. Hemscott Hill Farm, Druridge Bay

- **Overview:** Bell tents and wild dune camping by the sea, plus meet the farm's alpacas.
- **Address:** Cresswell NE61 5EQ
- **Cost:** From £65/night.
- **Pro tip:** Try their dusk alpaca walks — they're an oddly calming company.

3. Hadrian's Wall Campsite

- **Overview:** Tents, pods, and caravans all just a mile from the wall.
- **Address:** Melkridge, Haltwhistle NE49 9PG
- **Cost:** From £20/night (tent pitch), pods from £60.
- **Pro tip:** Walk to Walltown Crags at sunrise — it's magical.

4. Springhill Farm Wigwams, Seahouses

- **Overview:** Heated timber pods close to the coast. Great for groups or families.
- **Address:** Seahouses NE68 7UR

- **Cost:** From £55/night.
- **Pro tip:** Bring marshmallows — there's a communal fire pit.

5. Middlemoor Farm Camping

- **Overview:** Simple grass pitches with panoramic views, plus a few quirky cabins.
- **Address:** North Charlton NE67 5HP
- **Cost:** From £15/tent, cabins from £70.
- **Pro tip:** Perfect for hitting Bamburgh and Seahouses without breaking the bank.

Why You'll Love Staying Here

Northumberland has this way of making even your nights part of the adventure — whether you're tucked under thick beams in a centuries-old inn, peering at the stars from a yurt porch, or padding across a cottage kitchen floor with a mug of tea at dawn.

And wherever you stay, there's a good chance you'll wake up to birdsong, a castle silhouette, or the smell of sea air. Honestly, what more could you want?

CHAPTER 11: ITINERARIES TO SUIT EVERY TRAVELER

Planning a trip to Northumberland is a bit like being handed a box of chocolates — there's so much good stuff you're not quite sure where to start.

Whether you're popping up for a weekend, indulging in a longer adventure, travelling with kids, your sweetheart, or just a battered backpack, these itineraries will help you shape the perfect Northumbrian escape.

3 Days in Northumberland: A Quick Escape

Perfect for: A long weekend break, first-timers, or those wanting a taste of it all.

Day 1 – Castles & Coast

- Morning: Explore **Alnwick Castle & Gardens**. Try the treehouse café for coffee.
- Afternoon: Drive to **Craster** for lunch on kippers and a breezy walk to **Dunstanburgh Castle**.
- Evening: Dinner at The Jolly Fisherman in Craster or back in Alnwick.

Day 2 – Bamburgh & Seahouses

- Morning: Tour **Bamburgh Castle**, wander the beach.
- Afternoon: Take a boat trip from Seahouses to the **Farne Islands** (April–July best for puffins).
- Evening: Fish and chips on Seahouses harbour, then stroll to watch the sunset.

Day 3 – A Touch of History

- Morning: Head inland to **Hadrian's Wall**. Walk from Steel Rigg to Sycamore Gap.
- Afternoon: Visit **Hexham Abbey**, then tea in the marketplace.
- Evening: Head home (reluctantly).

Pro Tip: Book castle tickets and boat tours in advance on weekends.

7-Day Classic Northumberland

Perfect for: Those wanting to dig deeper into the landscapes, coast, castles, and villages.

Day 1 – Alnwick & Alnmouth

Arrive, settle in Alnwick. Explore the castle and gardens, then drive to **Alnmouth** for a sandy stroll.

Day 2 – Coastal Trail

Start in **Craster**, walk to **Dunstanburgh**, continue to **Low Newton** for a pint at the Ship Inn.

Day 3 – Bamburgh & Holy Island

Morning at **Bamburgh Castle**, afternoon tide-dependent trip to **Lindisfarne**. Watch for the tide times!

Day 4 – Seahouses & Farne Islands

Morning boat trip to see puffins, seals. Afternoon around Seahouses shops and beaches.

Day 5 – Hadrian's Wall Country

Full day exploring the wall: **Vindolanda, Housesteads**, scenic walks. Pub dinner near Hexham.

Day 6 – Cheviot Hills & Wooler

Walk a gentle Cheviot trail, then browse Wooler's village shops. Stop for cake at a local tearoom.

Day 7 – Rothbury & Cragside

Spend your final day at **Cragside House & Gardens**, then wander Rothbury before heading home.

Pro Tip: Base yourself in two places (e.g., Alnwick + Hexham) to avoid long daily drives.

Romantic Getaway for Couples

Perfect for: Slow mornings, hand-in-hand walks, and secret scenic spots.

Day 1 – Coastal Dreams

Stay in a seaside cottage or boutique inn. Explore **Alnmouth**, have seafood at the Hope & Anchor.

Day 2 – Castles & Kisses

Tour **Bamburgh Castle**, then picnic on the dunes. Wander Seahouses harbour by sunset.

Day 3 – Lindisfarne

Drive across the causeway to **Holy Island**, visit the priory and castle, then toast with local mead.

Day 4 – Dark Skies

Head to **Kielder Water & Observatory**. Book a stargazing session — it's wildly romantic under a billion stars.

Pro Tip: Spring and autumn are quieter, still beautiful, and you'll have beaches almost to yourselves.

Family Fun Itinerary with Kids

Perfect for: Explorers of all ages who need a mix of castles, creatures, and ice creams.

Day 1 – Bamburgh & Beach

Morning castle adventures, sandcastle building in the afternoon. Easy dinner in Seahouses.

Day 2 – Farne Islands

Boat trip to see seals and puffins (kids love this). Fish & chips by the water.

Day 3 – Alnwick

Morning broomstick training (Harry Potter fans!) at Alnwick Castle. Afternoon maze and fountains in the gardens.

Day 4 – Hauxley Wildlife & Druridge Bay

Wildlife spotting, beach play, maybe kite flying. Evening back at your cottage or park lodge.

Day 5 – Hadrian's Wall

Short, kid-friendly walks. Vindolanda has live archaeology that fascinates little minds.

Pro Tip: Pack spare clothes — between beaches, boat spray, and muddy ruins, someone's bound to get grubby.

Senior-Friendly Relaxed Journey

Perfect for: Travellers who want less climbing, more gentle wandering and cultural stops.

Day 1 – Alnwick & Market Town Life

Alnwick Castle & Gardens with plenty of sitting spots. Browse shops and antique stores.

Day 2 – Coastal Villages

Drive to Craster, enjoy smoked fish, gentle stroll to Dunstanburgh viewpoint. Continue to Low Newton.

Day 3 – Hexham & Hadrian's Wall

Abbey tour, slow café lunch, then short walks at Walltown Crags.

Day 4 – Rothbury & Cragside

Tour house interiors, gardens, and riverside teas in Rothbury.

Pro Tip: Choose central hotels to reduce driving — many offer lifts and accessible rooms.

Backpacker's Budget Itinerary

Perfect for: Hostel-hoppers with hiking boots, a railcard, and no fear of weather.

Day 1 – Alnwick

Stay at Alnwick Youth Hostel. Self-cater meals. Tour castle (student discounts available).

Day 2 – Craster to Seahouses Hike

Start in Craster, a coastal walk past Dunstanburgh to Seahouses. Fish & chips for fuel.

Day 3 – Bamburgh

Bus or hitchhike to Bamburgh. Cheap lunch from a bakery, explore the beach and castle from outside if saving pennies.

Day 4 – Berwick

Train to Berwick, explore old town walls, cheap eats at a riverside café.

Day 5 – Hadrian's Wall

Stay at Hexham Hostel. Walk a wall section with packed sandwiches from the market.

Pro Tip: Megabus to Newcastle + local buses = very wallet-friendly way to cover ground.

Photographer's Trail: Castles, Wildlife, and Landscapes

Perfect for: Travellers who chase the golden hour and stand in mud for *that* shot.

Day 1 – Bamburgh at Dawn

Get to the beach for sunrise silhouettes of the castle. Move to Seahouses for boat trips — seals make great subjects.

Day 2 – Holy Island & Craster

Cross the causeway early, catch Lindisfarne Castle in soft morning light. Afternoon in Craster for coastal shots.

Day 3 – Cheviot Hills

Hike Yeavering Bell for vast panoramas. Keep wide lenses ready.

Day 4 – Hadrian's Wall

Golden hour at Sycamore Gap, then astro shots if it's clear.

Day 5 – Kielder Dark Skies

Evening at the Observatory for Milky Way photography.

Pro Tip: Always check tide times for Lindisfarne and weather forecasts for the wall. Wet kit = grumpy photographer.

Why These Itineraries Work

The beauty of Northumberland is it's flexibility. Want to swap castles for gardens? Or pubs for wildlife centres? Easy. These itineraries give you a framework, but the real magic comes from all the little detours and café stops along the way.

CHAPTER 12: NORTHUMBERLAND FOR EVERY SEASON

If you ask locals when's the best time to visit Northumberland, most will give you a cheeky smile and say, *"All of them."*

They're not wrong. Each season changes the character of this place completely. In spring it's alive with birdsong and blossoms. Come summer, the coastline hums with energy and laughter. By autumn it slows, cloaked in rich colour. And winter? That's when you find the real hush — snowy castles, ghost stories by the fire, and empty beaches that feel all yours.

Let me walk you through the pleasures of each season here, so you can decide what suits your mood best.

Spring: Blossoms, Birds & Coastal Breezes

Ah, spring. The hedgerows burst with frothy hawthorn, lambs wobble on unsteady legs, and the days stretch longer, teasing you to stay out past supper.

What to do:

- Walk the riverside at **Warkworth**, watching ducklings paddle by.
- Spot puffins returning to nest on the **Farne Islands** (late April onwards).

- Visit **Alnwick Garden** when the cherry orchard is a pink wonderland.

Why it's special: There's a freshness to everything. Even the castles seem to sit up a little taller under soft new leaves.

- **Pro tip:** Bring layers. A sunny morning can still turn into a bracing afternoon that'll have you wishing for a bobble hat.

Summer: Festivals, Hikes & Sea Adventures

Long daylight hours mean you can pack in twice as much exploring — or just linger over pints outside a pub with the sun on your back.

What to do:

- Join a boat trip from Seahouses to see seals, puffins, maybe even dolphins.
- Hike a full day on **Hadrian's Wall** or up into the **Cheviots** with picnic breaks.
- Check out local fairs and markets — there's usually a festival or food event every weekend somewhere.

Why it's special: Wildflowers flood the dunes, kids shriek in rockpools, and the villages feel properly alive. Evenings often stretch to near 10pm — perfect for after-dinner beach strolls.

- **Pro tip:** Book accommodation well ahead, especially in school holidays. And yes, still pack a raincoat — it's still England.

Autumn: Foliage, Peace & Stargazing

By September the crowds thin, the pace slows, and the countryside dresses itself in gold, copper, and ruby.

What to do:

- Wander through **Cragside's woodlands** or **Rothbury riverside**, leaves crunching underfoot.
- Visit **Kielder Observatory** for stargazing under some of the darkest skies in Europe.
- Cosy up in a stone pub after a breezy coastal walk — nothing beats hot pie when the wind picks up.

Why it's special: It feels like Northumberland takes a deep breath. There's a quiet romance in the lanes, and you might have entire beaches to yourself.

- **Pro tip:** Shorter days meal plan walks early, and keep a torch handy if you find yourself chasing sunsets a bit too long.

Winter: Snowy Castles, Quiet Trails & Firelit Pubs

If you want true stillness — frosty hedges, silent castle walls, and pubs lit up against early dusk — winter is when to come.

What to do:
Visit **Bamburgh or Alnwick Castle** dusted with snow — they look like something out of a fairytale.

- Take bracing walks on empty beaches. Seahouses and Beadnell are hauntingly beautiful in winter light.
- Find a pub with a roaring fire and stay for slow lunches that turn into early suppers.

Why it's special: You'll often have famous spots nearly to yourself. And there's nothing quite like wrapping cold hands around a steaming mug after a walk that's left your cheeks stinging.

- **Pro tip:** Some smaller attractions close or have shorter hours — always check ahead. Bring sturdy boots and watch for icy patches.
Why Every Season's Worth It

Truth is, Northumberland is one of those rare places that suits any mood, any month. Spring and summer if you want life and energy, autumn for reflection and colour, winter for stories by the hearth and frost-kissed silence.

CHAPTER 13: EVENTS, FESTIVALS & LOCAL TRADITIONS

You can spend days in Northumberland utterly content just wandering castles and coastlines. But time it right, and you'll catch this county at its most festive, alive with lantern-lit gardens, medieval revelry, proud farming traditions, and even the slightly daft delight of watching puffins clumsily take off from cliff edges.

If your dates are flexible, consider tying your trip to one of these local gems. Here are some of my favourite annual highlights — each a window into Northumberland's big heart and playful spirit.

Alnwick Garden Illuminations

When: Late October through early January
Where: Alnwick Garden, Alnwick NE66 1YU
Cost: Around £15 adult, £8 child (prices vary by day)

Every winter, as the days shrink and the air nips your nose, the Alnwick Garden transforms into a glowing wonderland. Twinkling light tunnels, lantern forests, cascading illuminated fountains — it's pure magic.

Last year I strolled through with a hot mulled wine, watching kids twirl under fairy lights and even the sternest grandparents beam like children. It's part art installation, part festive fairground, and utterly joyful.

Pro tip: Book evening slots early, especially close to Christmas, and wear warm boots — it gets chilly on those garden paths.

Lindisfarne Gospels Festival

When: Typically runs in summer or early autumn in special years when the Gospels are displayed. Check listings.
Where: Various venues including Holy Island, Berwick, Alnwick.

When the priceless **Lindisfarne Gospels** (a masterpiece of Anglo-Saxon art) return to the North East on exhibition tours, it sparks festivals of music, crafts, medieval fairs, and special church services.

Even if the Gospels themselves aren't on display locally that year, Lindisfarne often hosts heritage days, with re-enactments and monks chanting in old priory ruins. It's haunting and beautiful.

Pro tip: If you're visiting Holy Island during any festival, *always* double-check tide times for the causeway — the sea waits for no one.

Farne Islands Puffin Watch (May–July)

When: Peak nesting from late May to late July
Where: Boat tours from Seahouses

Every spring, thousands of puffins flap in from sea to lay eggs on the Farne Islands. Their clownish faces, bright beaks, and comical crash-landings never fail to delight — I could watch them for hours.

Boat operators like **Serenity Boats** or **Billy Shiel's** offer dedicated puffin tours, often including grey seals basking on rocks too.

Pro tip: Bring a decent camera or binoculars, and a hat — gulls get very 'enthusiastic' if you walk too close to nests. Trust me on this.

Northumberland County Show

When: Late May bank holiday
Where: Bywell Hall, near Stocksfield NE43 7AB
Cost: Around £12 adult, under 16s free

If you want the full rural flavour of Northumberland, this is it: prize cattle gleaming in the sun, sheepdog trials, show-jumping, artisan food tents, and kids with ice cream smeared all over their faces.

It's old-school, heartwarming fun — plus a brilliant chance to sample local cheeses, pies, and fudge straight from the producers.

Pro tip: Wear boots. Even on dry days, you'll find yourself in fields with mud that loves to claim city shoes.

Berwick Film & Media Arts Festival

When: Usually late September
Where: Various venues around Berwick-upon-Tweed

A quirky international film festival set within the medieval ramparts of Berwick, mixing cinema with live art and surprise pop-up performances.

One year I found myself watching a short film projected inside an old warehouse while a cellist played beside us — you never quite know what's next.

Pro tip: Stay over in Berwick. Wandering the old town walls between shows is half the fun.

Local Christmas Markets

When: Late November through December
Where: Alnwick, Hexham, Morpeth, Berwick and more

Nothing quite like the smell of mulled cider, roasting chestnuts, and stalls piled with handmade wreaths and woollen hats.

- **Alnwick Market Square** lights up with festive stalls under the glow of the castle.
- **Hexham Abbey's Christmas fair** is delightfully Dickensian.
- **Morpeth's market** mixes local food producers with carol singers.

Pro tip: Most run weekends only. Go later in the afternoon to see twinkling lights turn on — magical with a hot chocolate in hand.

Why These Events Matter

Big or small, these gatherings stitch communities together, letting you peek behind the postcard scenery into real local life. You'll swap nods with farmers who've brought prize sheep, kids chasing candy floss, artists fussing with light rigs — all sharing the same square, the same stories.

It's this cheerful tapestry of tradition that makes Northumberland so deeply lovable, whether you're watching a puffin take off or standing by a roaring fire after a frosty walk.

CHAPTER 14: DAY TRIPS BEYOND NORTHUMBERLAND

As much as I could spend eternity pottering around Northumberland's coast, castles, and country pubs, there's no denying its brilliant location for quick hops into other gems of northern England and southern Scotland.

If you've carved out a longer stay, these day trips add even more colour to your adventure — each just close enough for a satisfying out-and-back without hauling your luggage.

Durham & Cathedral Day Trip

Travel time: Around 1 hour 15 by car from Alnwick, or 1 hour 30 by train from Berwick or Alnmouth (with a Newcastle change).

Why go:
Durham is one of England's most spectacular small cities, wrapped in a loop of the River Wear. Its **cathedral**, a UNESCO World Heritage Site, is so magnificent that when I first stepped inside I nearly dropped my sandwich.

- Wander through the soaring nave that doubled as Hogwarts in the early Harry Potter films.

- Climb the cathedral tower (325 steps if your knees allow) for sweeping views.
- Explore the winding cobbled streets below, stuffed with book shops and tearooms.

Pro tip: Pop into **Vennel's Café** for homemade cakes tucked down a medieval alleyway. The fruit scones are scandalously good.

Edinburgh from Berwick-upon-Tweed

Travel time: Only 45 minutes by direct train from Berwick-upon-Tweed.

Why go: Fancy breakfast by Bamburgh's dunes, lunch under Edinburgh Castle? Northumberland makes that dream surprisingly doable.

- Stroll the **Royal Mile**, dipping into whisky shops and tartan boutiques.
- Visit the **National Museum of Scotland** (free!).
- Snap that classic Edinburgh Castle shot from Princes Street Gardens.
- Or just get gloriously lost in the tangle of Old Town closes.

Pro tip: Advance LNER train tickets can be as cheap as £10-15 each way if you book early. Sit on the east side heading north for sea cliff views.

Hadrian's Wall & The Lake District Border

Travel time: About 90 minutes from Hexham to Keswick (the northern Lake District).

Why go: Already exploring Hadrian's Wall? It's tempting to keep going west. Soon the rugged Roman frontier melts into the lush valleys of the Lake District.

- Grab coffee in **Keswick**, pick up Herdwick lamb pies at the market, then wander Derwentwater's shore.
- Short on time? Even driving through the passes is worth it for jaw-dropping scenery.

Pro tip: Check weather forecasts obsessively — lakes mean sudden showers. A bright start can turn to monsoon before your second scone.

Tynemouth & Newcastle Coastal Break

Travel time: Just over an hour from Alnwick by car, or 90 minutes by bus/train combo.

Why go: Maybe you fancy a day that blends fresh sea air with urban energy. Tynemouth is a vibrant coastal town at the mouth of the Tyne, and Newcastle's just upriver.

- In **Tynemouth**, explore the ruined priory perched above Longsands Beach.

- Browse antiques at the station market (weekends).
- Then head into **Newcastle** for riverside art at the BALTIC or a stroll over the Millennium Bridge.

Pro tip: If you love fish and chips, Riley's Fish Shack on King Edward's Bay serves them straight from a wood-fired oven, feet from the sand. Expect queues — it's that good.

Why These Day Trips Are Perfect

They're close enough to feel easy, far enough to feel like a fresh adventure. Plus, each one lets you bring a slice of somewhere new back to your Northumberland base — a bit of Scottish poetry, some Cumbrian fudge, or tales of Newcastle nightlife.

And you'll be back by evening, ready to collapse into a local pub with stories of yet another perfect day.

EXCLUSIVE BONUS

Legends, Ghosts & Quirky Tales of Northumberland

No true Northumberland adventure is complete without a few shivers up the spine — or a knowing grin at the county's delightfully odd history.
After all, this is a land of ancient battlegrounds, smugglers' caves, windswept ruins, and lonely roads where locals still give a cautious nod to "things you best not laugh at."

So pour yourself a local ale (or something stronger), lean a bit closer to the fire, and let me share a few of my favourite ghost stories, legends, and local oddities.

The Grey Lady of Bamburgh

Bamburgh Castle may look majestic by day, perched proudly above the crashing North Sea — but once the sun dips, tales swirl of the **Grey Lady**.

Some say she was a noblewoman who threw herself from the battlements, despairing over a lost love. Others whisper she simply vanished in a storm, her spirit condemned to forever walk the windswept walls.

More than one night porter has reported seeing a pale figure gliding along the ramparts, vanishing when challenged. Visitors who find the wind oddly warm for a moment sometimes joke, "It's just her passing by." But only half in jest.

Chillingham Castle's Blue Boy

Now if you want *proper* haunted, **Chillingham Castle** has been dubbed the most haunted in Britain — and the owners proudly market it that way.

Most famous is the **Blue Boy**, once often seen in the Pink Room (the names here are delightfully contradictory). Guests reported waking to hear wails and to see a blue halo above their bed. Centuries-old walls were eventually opened, revealing the skeletal remains of a child and scraps of blue cloth.

These days, the cries are rarer, but night tours still promise cold spots, rattling doors, and one or two nervous giggles that definitely don't come from the guides.

The Headless Horseman of Warkworth

Not to be outdone, **Warkworth Castle** boasts its own grim legend: a spectral horseman galloping through the grounds without a head.

Locals say it's the ghost of Sir Bertram de Bothal, who mistakenly killed his own lover in a fit of rage, then rode out to die in remorse. On stormy nights, people swear they've seen a dark shape racing the castle walls, hooves pounding where no horse should be.

Sycamore Gap's Lost Roman Legion

Even the serene Sycamore Gap on Hadrian's Wall — that iconic lone tree — has stories to unsettle. Some hikers have reported hearing the faint clang of armour, or voices barking orders in Latin, only to turn and find the path empty.

Legend says a Roman cohort was ambushed nearby, and doomed to endlessly patrol their old frontier. Or maybe it's just the wind funnelling through the gap — though sometimes, on a grey dusk, I'm not so sure.

Smugglers' Tunnels & Vanishing Pints

Northumberland's coast was notorious for smuggling — wool, brandy, tobacco, you name it.
 Villages like **Craster** and **Seahouses** still have stories of secret tunnels leading from cliffside caves to old inns, where a wink and a coin might get you "a special brew."

Today, those tunnels are mostly blocked or forgotten. But locals love to tell tales of barrels rolling by themselves at night, or pints that mysteriously empty when no one's touched them. Personally, I blame a thirsty past rather than a ghostly one. But it makes for a good story over the bar.

Why We Keep Telling These Tales

Maybe it's the long winter nights, or the mists that roll so thick you can barely see the next hedgerow. Maybe it's just that Northumberland has lived through so many centuries, it can't help collecting a few extra souls along the way.

Either way, these stories add a delicious tingle to castle corridors and windswept lanes. So next time you feel a sudden chill in a sunlit room, or hear footsteps behind you on a woodland path — don't worry. It's probably just the past saying hello.

Before You Sleep...

If you're travelling with children (or the faint-hearted), remind them these are only tales... mostly.

And if you're sleeping over at Chillingham or anywhere near Warkworth, perhaps leave a little lamp on. Just to be sure.

CONCLUSION

Until We Meet in Northumberland

So here we are at the end of these pages — though if I've done my job right, it's only the beginning of your Northumberland story.

Whether you've been drawn in by castles perched on cliffs, windswept beaches where the only footprints might be your own, or the quiet joy of finding a tiny village tearoom after a long walk, Northumberland has a way of sneaking into your heart. It certainly did mine.

This corner of England is rich in contrasts: grand histories and simple pleasures, dramatic landscapes and gentle smiles from strangers you'll meet along the way. It's a place that hums with the ghosts of Romans, rebels, monks, miners — and yet somehow still feels undiscovered enough that you'll often have it all to yourself.

When you come (because I hope you do), don't rush. Let the tides, the weather, and the moods of the day set your pace. Wander without too many plans. Stop when you see a bench with a view, or a pub with a crooked sign promising a roaring fire.

And if you find yourself alone at twilight near an old stone wall or under the canopy of a vast night sky —

pause, breathe it in. You're sharing it with countless souls who've stood right there before you, marveling at how a place can feel both timeless and entirely yours in that moment.

So here's to you and your upcoming Northumberland adventures. May your days be full of sunlight (or at least dramatic clouds for your photos), your boots muddied in the best possible way, and your evenings spent recounting the day's discoveries over something hearty and local.

Safe travels — and who knows? Perhaps our paths will cross on some narrow lane or castle rampart. I'll be the one grinning like a fool at it all.

Northumberland Travel Guide 2025-2025

MAPS

Northumberland Map

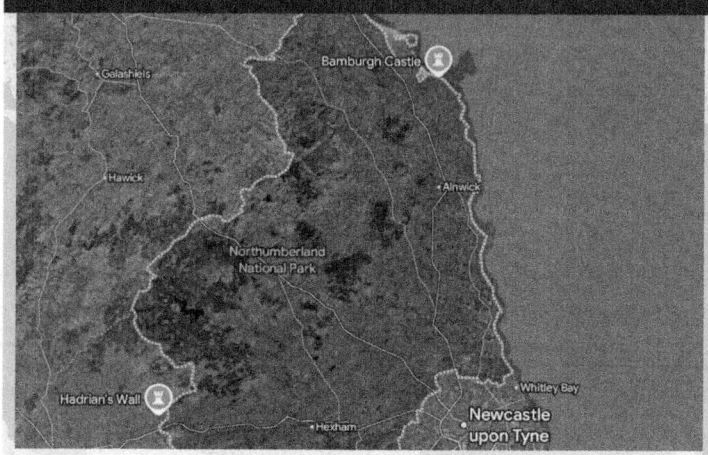

HOW TO SCAN

1. Open your smartphone's camera app.
2. Point the camera at the QR code.
3. Hold the camera steady until your phone recognizes the QR code.
4. Tap the notification or link that appears to open the interactive map.
5. Explore the map and its features!

Northumberland Travel Guide 2025-2025

Bamburgh Castle Map	Alnwick Castle Map
Hadrian's Wall Map	Holy Island of Lindisfarne Map
Dunstanburgh Castle Coastal Walk Map	Sycamore Gap Map

Northumberland Travel Guide 2025-2025

Farne Islands Map	Northumberland National Park Map
Warkworth Village Map	Warkworth Castle Map
Chillingham Castle Map	The Cheviot Hills Map

Printed in Dunstable, United Kingdom